The Norwich School: John Old Crome, John Sell Cotman, George Vincent, James Stark, J. Berney Crome, John Thirtle, R. Ladbrooke, David Hodgson

Herbert Minton Cundall

THE
NORWICH SCHOOL

JOHN (" OLD") CROME, JOHN SELL COTMAN
GEORGE VINCENT, JAMES STARK
J. BERNEY CROME, JOHN THIRTLE
R. LADBROOKE, DAVID HODGSON
M. E. & J. J. COTMAN
ETC.

WITH ARTICLES BY H. M. CUNDALL, I.S.O., F.S.A.

1920

EDITED BY GEOFFREY HOLME
"THE STUDIO," LTD., LONDON, PARIS, NEW YORK

CONTENTS
ARTICLES BY H. M. CUNDALL, I.S.O., F.S.A.

	PAGE
Introduction	I
John Crome	8
John Sell Cotman	17
Other Members of the Norwich School	25

ILLUSTRATIONS IN COLOURS

		PLATE
Cotman, John Sell		
Greta Bridge, Yorkshire	(water-colour)	xxxvii
Mont St. Michel	,, ,,	xl
Ruined Castle near a Stream	,, ,,	xliii
Boats on Cromer Beach	(oil painting)	xlviii
Crome, John		
The Return of the Flock—Evening	(oil painting)	v
The Gate	,, ,,	x
A Bathing Scene—View on the Wensum at Thorpe, Norwich	(oil painting)	xv
Road with Pollards	,, ,,	xx

ILLUSTRATIONS IN MONOTONE

Cotman, John Joseph		
Whitlingham, looking towards Norwich	(water-colour)	lxxvii
Cotman, John Sell		
Bridge, Valley, and Mountain	,, ,,	xxxiii
Llangollen	,, ,,	xxxiv
Bridge at Saltram, Devonshire	,, ,,	xxxv
Durham Castle and Cathedral	,, ,,	xxxvi
Windmill in Lincolnshire	,, ,,	xxxviii
Dieppe	,, ,,	xxxix
Powis Castle	,, ,,	xli
The Palais de Justice and the Rue St. Lô, Rouen	,, ,,	xlii
Statue of Charles I, Charing Cross	,, ,,	xliv
Cader Idris	,, ,,	xlv
Eton College	,, ,,	xlvi
Study	,, ,,	xlvii
Boys Fishing	(oil painting)	xlix
House in the Place de la Pucelle at Rouen	(etching)	l
Château at Fontaine-le-Henri, near Caen	,,	li
Millbank on the Thames	,,	lii

v

ILLUSTRATIONS IN MONOTONE—Continued   PLATE

Cotman, Miles Edmund
    Boats on the Medway . . . . (oil painting) lxxv
    Trowse Mills . . . . . ,, ,, lxxvi

Crome, John
    Landscape . . . . . ,, ,, ii
    View on the Wensum . . . . ,, ,, iii
    Mousehold Heath, near Norwich . . ,, ,, iv
    Moonlight on the Yare . . . ,, ,, vi
    Landscape : Grove Scene . . . ,, ,, vii
    The Grove Scene, Marlingford . . ,, ,, viii
    The Village Glade . . . . ,, ,, ix
    Back of the New Mills, Norwich . . ,, ,, xi
    Cottage near Lakenham . . . ,, ,, xii
    Mill near Lakenham . . . . ,, ,, xiii
    On the Skirts of the Forest . . . ,, ,, xiv
    Back River, Norwich . . . . ,, ,, xvi
    Bruges River, Ostend in the Distance ;
        Moonlight . . . . . ,, ,, xvii
    Yarmouth Harbour . . . . ,, ,, xviii
    Boulevard des Italiens, Paris, 1814 . ,, ,, xix
    Yarmouth Jetty . . . . . ,, ,, xxi
    Blacksmith's Shop, near Hingham, Norfolk ,, ,, xxii
    Woody Landscape at Colney . . . ,, ,, xxiii
    Fishmarket on the Beach at Boulogne . ,, ,, xxiv
    Thatched Buildings . . . . (water-colour) xxv
    Lane Scene near Norwich . . . ,, ,, xxvi
    Landscape near Lakenham . . . ,, . ,, xxvii
    Maltings on the Wensum . . . ,, ,, xxviii
    Landscape with Figures . . . ,, ,, xxix
    Waiting for the Ferry . . . . ,, ,, xxx
    Woodland Scene, Dunham, Norfolk . ,, ,, xxxi
    Pencil Study xxxii

Crome, John Berney
    View near Bury St. Edmunds . . (oil painting) lxii
    River Scene by Moonlight . . . ,, ,, lxiii

Dixon, Robert
    The Farmyard . . . . (water-colour) lxxiv

Hodgson, David
    Old Fish Market, Norwich . . (oil painting) lxvi
  vi

Ladbrooke, John Berney
    Landscape . . . . . (oil painting) lxiv
    The Sluice Gate . . . . . ,, ,, lxv

Ladbrooke, Robert
    Beach Scene, Mundesley . . . ,, ,, lxi

Lound, Thomas
    Ely Cathedral . . . . . (water-colour) lxxviii
    St. Benet's Abbey . . . . (oil painting) lxxix

Ninham, Henry
    Fishgate Street, Norwich . . . ,, ,, lxvii

Opie, John, R.A.
    John Crome . . . . . ,, ,, i

Priest, Alfred
    Godstow Bridge, Oxford . . . ,, ,, lxxx

Stannard, Alfred
    Yarmouth Jetty . . . . . ,, ,, lxix

Stannard, Joseph
    Fishing Boats . . . . . ,, ,, lxviii

Stark, James
    Whitlingham, from Old Thorpe Grove . ,, ,, liii
    Thorpe Wood . . . . . ,, ,, liv
    Sheep Washing . . . . . ,, ,, lv
    Landscape with Cattle . . . . ,, ,, lvi
    The Forest Gate . . . . . ,, ,, lvii

Thirtle, John
    Whitlingham Reach . . . (water-colour) lxx
    Cromer, looking East . . . . ,, ,, lxxi
    View under Bishop's Bridge, Norwich . ,, ,, lxxii
    St. Magnus's Church, London Bridge, and
        neighbouring Buildings . . . ,, ,, lxxiii

Vincent, George
    Whitlingham, looking towards Norwich . (oil painting) lviii
    Trowse Meadows, near Norwich . . ,, ,, lix
    Cottage and Well . . . . ,, ,, lx

THE EDITOR DESIRES TO EXPRESS HIS THANKS TO MR. RUSSELL J. COLMAN, MR. H. DARELL-BROWN, MR. J. H. GURNEY, COLONEL SIR GEORGE LINDSAY HOLFORD, K.C.V.O., MR. R. W. LLOYD, MR. JOHN H. McFADDEN, MR. A. P. OPPÉ, MRS. LOUIS RAPHAEL, MR. ARTHUR MICHAEL SAMUEL, M.P., AND MR. F. W. SMITH WHO HAVE KINDLY ALLOWED WORKS OF THE NORWICH SCHOOL IN THEIR POSSESSION TO BE REPRODUCED HEREIN. HE ALSO WISHES TO ACKNOWLEDGE HIS INDEBTEDNESS TO MESSRS. THOS. AGNEW AND SONS, MR. E. G. CUNDALL, MR. FRANK LENEY, CURATOR OF THE CASTLE MUSEUM, NORWICH, AND THE AUTHORITIES OF THE BRITISH AND OF THE VICTORIA AND ALBERT MUSEUMS FOR THE VALUABLE ASSISTANCE THEY HAVE RENDERED IN THE PREPARATION OF THIS VOLUME.

INTRODUCTION

"THIS illustrious citizen was born in a tavern in the parish of St. George Tombland, and was buried in St. George Colegate. He was the founder of the 'Norwich School of Artists,' and his works, for which during his lifetime he seldom received more than a few pounds, are eagerly sought for by collectors, and in February 1913 his oil painting known as *The Willows* was sold in New York for eleven thousand pounds. Borrow, in 'Lavengro,' speaks of Crome as 'The little dark man with the brown coat and the top-boots, whose name will one day be considered the chief ornament of the old town, and whose works will at no distant period rank among the proudest pictures of England—and England against the world!'" Thus wrote the Lord Mayor of Norwich in convening a meeting of its citizens and others, held at the Castle Museum, to consider a fitting celebration next year of the centenary of John, or "Old" Crome, who died on April 22, 1821.

The Lord Mayor remarked at the meeting that there were still a great many people who did not know much about the Norwich School. Naturally lovers of art did, but he feared the great mass of people knew very little about the subject. This statement is undoubtedly true, and it may be a fitting opportunity for giving some account of the founder of the Norwich School and those associated with him. The works of the two principal leaders of this school—namely, John Crome and John Sell Cotman—are well-known to all connoisseurs, and numerous biographical notices and reviews have appeared concerning these two painters; those of the other men, however, attached to the movement have hardly obtained any recognition and are comparatively unknown.

In former days Norwich to a great extent owed its prosperity to its trade with Holland. Great Yarmouth was the principal port, and through it many paintings by Dutch masters found their way into the homes of prosperous merchants of the city. These pictures may have infused into the minds of the young men the idea of becoming painters, for at the beginning of the nineteenth century there were numerous striving young artists who chiefly gained their livelihood by teaching drawing.

To Norwich is due the honour of being the first city to establish an art school in England. The word 'school' is here used not in the ordinary scholastic term, but to denote a body of persons who are disciples of the same master, or who are united by a general similarity of principles and methods; it also means those whose training was obtained in the same locality, and implies more or less community of doctrine and styles. In addition to the founding of a school, Norwich may be accredited with having formed the first art club in the provinces. The Norwich Society was founded by John Crome in 1803 "for the purpose of an Enquiry into the Rise, Progress and present State of Painting, Architecture, and Sculpture, with a view to point out the Best Methods of Study to attain the Greater Perfection in these Arts." Its first meetings were held at a tavern called "The Hole in the Wall," in the parish of St. Andrew, where papers were read, followed by discussions, on subjects included in their inexhaustive programme. Two years later the Society removed to Sir Benjamin Wrench's Court, an old house which in the previous century had been the abode of a physician of that name. Here the Society may be said to have developed into an art club, for its members were allowed to have the use of the rooms as a studio, provided that they paid a fee for candles and firing if required ; and "bread-and-cheese" suppers were partaken of on evenings when meetings were held. In the year 1805 it was decided that the Society should hold its first exhibition in its own rooms. It was opened "as an encouragement and stimulus to Art and an educator of the public." It met with such success that the exhibition was held annually, under the name of the "Norwich Society of Artists," at Sir Benjamin Wrench's Court until the year 1825, when the building was demolished in order to make way for a new Corn Exchange. The exhibitions were revived three years later under the title of "The Norfolk and Suffolk Institution for the Promotion of the Fine Arts," and were continued for five years in a gallery called the "Artists' Room" specially built for the purpose in Exchange Street, not far from the old premises. The success of the Norwich Society was entirely due to two men, John Crome and John Sell Cotman. The former, who lived all his life in Norwich, with his *bonhomie* attracted many friends and pupils. He was undoubtedly the leading spirit of the movement until his death in 1821. After that date his mantle fell on Cotman, who continued to keep the Society together until he finally left Norwich for London to take up the position of drawing-master at King's College School. The Society, having lost its leader, ceased to exist.

Much has been written with regard to the relationship between Crome and Cotman. One writer asserts "a whole world lies between them "; another states they had little in common and socially "they were in different worlds," and lays emphasis on the difference between their ages. As the latter went to London to study art when about sixteen years of age, it is probable that there was little intercourse between them up to that time. Cotman, however, when he returned to reside in Norwich was a grown man of twenty-four years old, whilst Crome was only thirty-seven, no great disparagement in age, especially as the younger man had had experience of life in London and had already exhibited two pictures at the Royal Academy. At this time they doubtless became friends, although of entirely different characters, the one of a jovial disposition, fond of his

2

glass and pipe with his boon companions at a tavern in the evenings, whilst the other was excitable and subject to periods of hilarity alternated with fits of depression. Cotman joined the Norwich Society in 1807, and three years later he was elected Vice-President, whilst Crome held the post of President. Moreover, Cotman made a portrait study of Crome. Mr. Roget, writing with respect to this period, states "Cotman cannot properly be called a pupil of Crome's, though in some phases of his art there is too much in common with that of the older painter to leave room for doubt as to the influence of that admirable artist. It appears that he must have exercised such influence more as a companion than as a teacher."

With regard to their social positions, Cotman may have had the advantage of birth and education; but in spite of the drawbacks in this respect, Crome was certainly one of Nature's gentlemen, and won the admiration of all with whom he came in contact. Mr. James Reeve writes: " Although Crome had not the early advantages in education, etc., that Cotman had, great credit is due to him for the way he educated and improved himself, and in mature life the society in which he moved was in some cases quite equal to that of Cotman. Their feeling for art was altogether different, but they must have had much in common and were good friends. Crome was more homely in his habits but fitted to mix with gentlemen, otherwise the Gurney family would not have made a companion of him for art alone." Crome was content to paint chiefly from nature, grove scenes with oaks, and views on Mousehold Heath being his favourite subjects. He varied his style but little during his life. His scenes on the *Boulevard des Italiens, Paris* (Plate XIX) and *Fishmarket on the Beach at Boulogne* (Plate XXIV), in both of which are groups of people, may be taken as exceptions, as he rarely put more than three or four figures into his landscapes. Cotman, on the other hand, possibly owing to his want of success, varied his style considerably. He always had a tendency towards architectural subjects, probably due to his intimate relations with Mr. Dawson Turner, the antiquarian. These he painted in water-colours and etched in large numbers. Whilst living at Yarmouth he devoted himself to seascapes, and from time to time he took up oil-painting. In spite of the difference between the two painters in the mode of treating their subjects, it is possible to trace the influence of the elder as a companion, as Mr. Roget states, in some of the landscapes of the younger man.

In addition to these two masters, the following were the principal artists who comprised the Norwich School: James Stark and George Vincent, both pupils of Crome, who founded their art on the principles of their master and their study of the Dutch landscape painters. The former artist, in the treatment and execution of his subjects, cannot be compared with Crome; but in spite of this there is a pleasing quietness in his landscapes, which at the present time are receiving the attention of art collectors. Vincent had far higher powers and produced a large picture, entitled *Greenwich Hospital*, which, when exhibited at the London International Exhibition, 1862, obtained for him a recognition of being a great landscape painter; unfortunately Vincent fell into difficulties and was lost sight of by the art world. John Berney Crome, the eldest son of "Old" Crome, became a successful painter under the guidance of his father. He frequently introduced moonlight effects into his paintings. Robert Ladbrooke was associated with Crome from his boyhood, and both marrying sisters increased the bond between them; there was, however, an episode which parted them. Owing to a quarrel Ladbrooke and his followers seceded from the Norwich Society of Artists in 1816 and started another exhibition, styled "The Norfolk and Norwich Society of Artists"; it only lasted for two years and most of his followers returned to the original Society; but the breach was never completely healed, for it was only after Crome's death that Ladbrooke again sent contributions to the parent Society. His two sons, Henry and John Berney, became painters. They were pupils of their uncle, "Old" Crome, and produced landscapes somewhat in imitation of their master. Miles Edmund and John Joseph Cotman both followed in their father's footsteps, but neither in any way approached him. John Thirtle (a miniaturist as well as a landscape painter), by marrying the sister of Cotman's wife, became closely associated with him and was doubtless influenced by him. David Hodgson, a son of Charles Hodgson, an architectural painter, chiefly produced views of picturesque houses and street scenes. Robert Dixon was a water-colour artist as well as a scene-painter; he also executed some soft-ground etchings. Thomas Lound was an accomplished amateur who painted landscapes in oil and water-colours.

Nearly all these artists followed the profession of a drawing-master, and to a considerable extent gained a living thereby. The polite arts of the young ladies of genteel families, after leaving school, were fancy needlework, making wax flowers, and receiving drawing lessons from masters who visited their homes for the purpose. It was fortunate for these men that the modern athletic girl was totally unknown, otherwise their means of livelihood, if it had not been for teaching in schools, would have been very precarious.

In the first part of the nineteenth century etching was practised to a great extent in Norwich, not only by artists, but also by amateurs. Dutch etchings, like paintings, were conveyed from Holland to the Eastern Counties, and these may possibly have given the inspiration for their

4

production. Crome only etched for his own gratification. He executed his etchings chiefly between the years 1809 and 1813, but none of them were published until after his death. Cotman produced a large number, mainly architectural, and those on soft-ground were admirably executed. With regard to the hard-ground etchings, according to his own statement, he was a follower of Piranesi. Henry Ninham, Robert Dixon, George Vincent, Joseph Stannard, and other artists worked with the etching-needle, but the most successful was the Rev. E. T. Daniell, who may be described as one of the foremost of the English painter-etchers. In the Reeve Collection at the British Museum are other etchings by Mrs. Dawson Turner and her daughters and E. and R. Girling.

In the year 1862 a considerable impetus was given to the Norwich School when the now celebrated *Mousehold Heath* by Crome, originally sold for one guinea, was exhibited at the International Exhibition, and acquired for the nation for four hundred times its original price. This was the first important painting of the School to be seen in a National Collection, for up to that time Crome had been only represented by two small oil paintings in the Sheepshanks Gift at the South Kensington Museum. Henceforward the works of Crome and his pupils found their way to London and their value greatly increased, especially in the case of the master. Considering the amount of his time occupied in teaching, their number must have been very limited, and it may safely be said that the works attributed to Crome at the present time must be far in excess of those actually painted by him. It was not until a later date that the works of Cotman received the recognition they deserved, and at the present time it may be difficult to say which of these two men stands in the higher position.

Attributions, which have been recklessly applied to the paintings of this particular School, have caused considerable controversy. The little diversity of the scenery around Norwich and the Norfolk broads, and the similarity in the choice of subjects by the pupils and their master, may in some manner account for mistaken nomenclature. In early life Crome studied the works of Wilson and Gainsborough, as drawings exhibited by him at the early exhibitions of the Norwich Society are described in the catalogues as being " after Wilson " and " in the style of Gainsborough "; but he was evidently more influenced by the Dutch masters. The two paintings, both named *Mousehold Heath*, one in the National Gallery and the other in the Victoria and Albert Museum, have a Cuyp-like effect; his few moonlight scenes may be compared with the work of Van der Neer; but it was Hobbema who mainly attracted Crome. Although to a certain extent under the influence of these men, Crome developed his own style, to which he adhered with little or no change throughout his life. He painted trees, especially the oak, in a manner peculiar to himself, and a study of his *Poringland Oak* in the National Gallery, showing the careful manner in which not only the leaves, but also the trunk of the tree are painted, will best explain his methods. It is somewhat remarkable that his pictures were only painted with the trees in leaf, chiefly with autumnal tints, and no winter scene was executed by him. James Stark has perhaps suffered most by the attribution of his best pictures to the hand of his master. One which was exhibited at a Royal Academy Winter Exhibition was described in the catalogue as being by Crome. The excellence of the work was pointed out by the art critics, and stated to be quite unapproachable by any of his pupils. On the other hand, feeble paintings with little resemblance to the Norwich School have been assigned to Stark. Works of both George Vincent and Crome's son, John Berney Crome, have been attributed to their master, and the two pupils have been confused one with the other. An important painting, *The Yarmouth Water Frolic*, was sold at Christie's some years ago for two thousand six hundred guineas as an " Old " Crome ; it was discovered subsequently to be the work of his son. A fine oil painting, *A View of Yarmouth from Gorleston*, now owned by Mr. Arthur Michael Samuel, M.P., was sold as being by John Berney Crome, but afterwards found to be a painting by George Vincent, as it bears his monogram "G. V." on the stem of a boat at the right-hand corner of the picture. Considerable doubt often exists with regard to the drawings of John Sell Cotman and his two sons, Miles Edmund and John Joseph. This may be chiefly attributed to the fact that the latter were taught by their father, and they all worked together in making studies for their pupils to copy, even Cotman's daughter, Ann, being called in to assist in this work. These studies were usually signed by Cotman, with no intention of passing them off as his own work, but merely as an identification of their being his property. Consequently there are many drawings in existence which, although bearing his signature, are not the work of the master. Neither of the sons possessed the genius of their father, nor did they have his poetic feeling, consequently in his important drawings, executed in a free and masterly manner, there is little difficulty in distinguishing his hand. With regard to his oil-paintings, as he executed but very few, and these only spasmodically, they are not so easily identified, and some controversy has taken place respecting several of them.

Norwich has always endeavoured to maintain its reputation as an art centre, and numerous art societies, under various titles, have been formed from time to time. In 1839 attempts were made to revive the Norwich Society of Artists, and an exhibition was held at St. Andrew's Broad Street, called the " Norfolk and Norwich Art Union," but it appears to have met with little success, for there was no other exhibition until three years later, when, under the title of the " East of England Art Union," one took place in the Exchange Street Rooms. During the years 1848 to 1860 the " Norfolk and Norwich Association for the Promotion of the Fine Arts" held exhibitions, and the last of them was devoted to the works of deceased local artists. In 1868 and following year the " Norwich, Fine Art Association" held exhibitions in the Artists' Rooms, Exchange Street, and St. Andrew's Broad Street respectively. The present art society, known as the " Norwich Art Circle," was first started in 1885, and held annual exhibitions in its rooms at the Old Bank of England Chambers in Queen Street until about the close of the last century. This Society does not lay claim to being purely local, as the membership is not restricted to residents in the city or county; but it fosters the memory of the old painters of the Norwich School, and successful loan exhibitions of the paintings and drawings of John Thirtle, James Stark, John Sell Cotman, the Rev. E. T. Daniell, and Henry Ninham were held in the years 1886 to 1888, 1891, and 1906. The illustrated catalogues, with memoirs of these respective painters, are most valuable records of their works. The lasting memorial, however, to John Crome and his followers is in the Norwich Castle Museum, where a valuable collection of their paintings is permanently placed. In 1876 a few ardent admirers of these men formed themselves into the " East Anglian Art Society" for the purpose of acquiring works of the Norwich School and of local painters of the present time. They were successful in securing a small collection of pictures—*View on the Wensum* by John Crome (Plate III), being one of them—which was handed over to the Corporation on the completion of the Castle Museum in 1894. This collection has since received an important addition by the splendid bequest of the late Mr. J. J. Colman. The most important record of the Norwich School is to be found in the British Museum. In 1902 a collection of drawings, etchings, and documents relating to it were acquired from Mr. James Reeve, the well-known authority on the subject. For many years he made a special study of the painters and their works, and his collection forms a most valuable history of a school which sprang into existence at Norwich at the commencement of the nineteenth century and lasted for thirty years. To this record the writer is indebted for much of the information which is given in the following articles; and to Mr. Charles J. Watson, R.E., another authority on the Norwich School, he tenders his best thanks for the valuable assistance he has so kindly rendered.

JOHN CROME

IT is remarkable that three of the most prominent British landscape painters were all natives of East Anglia. Gainsborough was born at Sudbury in Suffolk; Constable at East Bergholt, only a few miles away; and Crome at Norwich. There is no romantic scenery to be found in the Eastern Counties to inspire an artist as there is in other districts of the British Isles; yet the quiet pastures in the valley of the Stour, and the Dutch-like views on the Norfolk Broads have their attractions for all lovers of nature. It is also remarkable that "Old" Crome, begot of obscure parents and receiving but little or no education, should have developed a School of Painting in a city where art, beyond the portraits of local worthies, had hitherto been almost unknown. John Crome was born on December 22, 1768, at a small ale-house named "The King and the Miller," situated in a district of Norwich known as the Castle Ditches. His father was a journeyman-weaver, but whether he kept the inn, or was only a lodger, is not certain. In those days boys and girls seeking work used to assemble on an open space where the Ducal Palace formerly stood, on the chance of finding an engagement. This was called "going on the Palace." Young Crome followed the example and was fortunate in obtaining employment under Dr. Rigby, a physician, who took him into his service as an errand boy. He remained with the worthy doctor for two years, and if the tales Crome was wont to narrate in later life are true, he played many a prank during his service, such as changing the labels attached to the medicine bottles—labels at that date were easily removed; they were not gummed on the bottle, but were strips of folded paper tied on with string, as frequently depicted in their sketches by Rowlandson and other caricaturists.

After leaving the doctor, Crome became apprenticed for seven years to Francis Whistler, a coach, house, and sign painter, of 41 Bethel Street. Here he learnt the rudiments of painting by grinding and mixing colours. He is credited with having painted numerous signboards for inns, and Mr. W. F. Dickes in "The Norwich School of Painting" gives illustrations of either side of "The Top Sawyer," which hung across Church Street in front of the inn. This training doubtless gave him the breadth of touch seen even in his early works. Whilst in the employ of the coach painter, Crome first became acquainted with Robert Ladbrooke, a youth about a year younger than himself. They both determined to be painters and became boon companions. According to Mr. Dawson Turner, they hired a garret which they converted into a studio, and owing to their poverty they had to struggle with continual difficulties to obtain materials for their work; it is said that Crome would often wander into the country with his colours and a piece of millboard to make sketches.

8

Apparently the two artists were able to sell some of their sketches to Messrs. Smith and Jaggars, printsellers at Norwich. Crome soon had the good fortune, probably through the printsellers, to come under the notice of Mr. Thomas Harvey of Catton, a prosperous citizen of Norwich. Besides being a collector of works of art, he was also an amateur artist. He invited Crome to his studio and gave him lessons in painting. He also allowed Crome to copy the pictures in his collection, amongst them the celebrated *Cottage Door* by Gainsborough and probably some works by Wilson, as in the exhibition of Crome's works held by the Norwich Society of Artists after his death in 1821, were two " compositions in the style of Richard Wilson " painted in 1796 and 1798 respectively. At Catton there were also numerous pictures by Dutch and Flemish painters, including a landscape by Hobbema which eventually passed into the hands of Mr. Dawson Turner, and was illustrated in his "Outlines in Lithography from a small Collection of Pictures," privately printed at Yarmouth in 1840.

Through Mr. Thomas Harvey, Crome became acquainted with Sir William Beechey, R.A., who, according to Edward Dayes the topographical painter, also began life as a house and sign painter, and John Chambers, in his "General History of the County of Norfolk," published in 1829, says a signboard by Beechey was still hanging in front of a village inn; another account states he was articled to an attorney in London, but obtained his release and gained admission to the schools of the Royal Academy. Anyhow, it is certain that Beechey went to reside at Norwich in 1781, and married Miss Jessop, a miniature painter. Five years later he returned to London, where he gained notoriety and royal patronage. Subsequently he paid occasional visits to his wife's birthplace, and it must have been during one of these that he met Crome, as Beechey wrote " Crome, when I first knew him, must have been about twenty years old, and was an awkward, uninformed country lad, but extremely shrewd in all his remarks upon art, though he wanted words and terms to express his meaning. As often as he came to town he never failed to call upon me and to get what information I was able to give him upon the subject of that particular branch of art which he had made his study. His visits were very frequent, and all his time was spent in my painting-room when I was not particularly engaged. He improved so rapidly that he delighted and astonished me. He always dined and spent his evenings with me."

From this statement it is evident Crome made frequent excursions to London, but at what dates it is not specified. As Beechey mentions that Crome sought his advice as to the best methods to pursue with regard to painting, it is probable that his early visits were made when he was a

9

young man, not sure of his powers. Be that as it may, the lure of the metropolis had no hold on him, for he always returned to his native city and its surrounding scenery.

John Opie, R.A., was another well-known painter to whom Crome owed some of his artistic education. Opie went to Norwich, as Beechey did, to paint portraits. He, too, found a wife there, as he married Miss Alderson, the daughter of a physician of the city. In a letter written by Mrs. Opie to Mr. Dawson Turner, she said " My husband was not acquainted with our friend, John Crome, before the year 1798, when we first visited Norwich after our marriage. Crome used frequently to come to my husband in Norwich ; and I have frequently seen him and Crome and our dear friend, Thomas Harvey, in the painting-room of the latter. I have also seen my husband painting for Crome ; that is, the latter looking on, while the former painted a landscape or figures. And, occasionally, I have seen him at work on Crome's own canvas, while the latter amused us with droll stories and humorous conversations and observations. But this is, to the best of my belief, the extent of *assistance* he derived from my husband."

Opie painted Crome's portrait (Plate I). It was given by Joseph, one of Crome's sons, to Mr. John Norgate of Norwich ; subsequently it passed into the possession of Mr. J. J. Colman, M.P., and was bequeathed by him to the Castle Museum. There is another portrait of Crome in the Guildhall, painted by Dr. Woodhouse. It was presented by Joseph Crome.

Much has been said with regard to Crome's poverty, but there is no direct evidence that he was ever in actual want. He worked hard to obtain a livelihood, and was not above continuing to paint signboards for inns even when thirty-five years of age ; for there exists a receipted bill for the sum of £2 4s. od., signed and dated John Crome, May 27, 1803, for " painting a ' Lame Dog ' and writing and gilding name on ' ye Maid's Head.' "

In 1792 Crome was in a position to marry. His wife was Phœbe Berney, or " Pheby Bearney," as she signed her name in the register. The wedding took place at St. Mary's Coslany on October 2nd of that year. There were reasons for this early marriage, as their first child, Abigail, was born on the 30th of the same month. Crome soon had a young and increasing family to maintain, which meant redoubling his efforts to support it.

It is probable it was on the advice of Mr. Thomas Harvey that Crome became a drawing-master, and possibly his first pupils were the daughters of Mr. John Gurney of Earlham. The following entry in the diary of Richenda Gurney is taken from " The Gurneys of Earlham," by Augustus J. C. Hare, " *Jan.* 17, 1798.—I had a good drawing this morning, but in

10

the course of it gave way to passion with both Crome and Betsy—Crome because he would attend to Betsy and not to me, and Betsy because she was so provoking." Through the introduction of two such influential patrons his circle of pupils greatly extended. In 1801 he was already living at 17 Gildengate Street (now St. George Street) as " John Crome, Drawing Master." He continued to live in this house and to give lessons in drawing until his death. It was Crome's practice to take his pupils into the country and to teach them to study direct from Nature. There is a story, told by Mr. John Wodderspoon, of a brother artist meeting Crome in a remote spot of healthy verdure with a troupe of young persons, and remarking, " Why, I thought I had left you in the city engaged in your school ! " " I am in my school," replied Crome, " and teaching my scholars from the only true examples. Do you think," pointing to a lovely distance, "that either you or I can do better than that ?" A similar anecdote is narrated in his book on " Landscape Painting " by John Burnet. " I remember," he says, " meeting my old friend, Mr. John Crome of Norwich (some of whose landscapes are not surpassed even by those of Gainsborough), with several of his pupils on the banks of the Yare. ' This is our academy,' he cried out triumphantly, holding up his brush." About this period Crome was appointed drawing-master at the Grammar School, which position he held for many years.

In the summer of the following year Mr. Gurney, with his son Samuel, six unmarried daughters and Mr. Fowell Buxton, made a tour of the Lake District ; Crome was taken with them. There are several references in the diaries of the young ladies respecting the artist during this tour. Hannah records, " *Ambleside*, 1802.—To-day we could not get out till rather late on account of the weather, which none of us minded, as we were all busily employed in drawing, Kitty reading to us. Chenda, Cilla, and Mr. Crome were comfortably seated in a romantic little summer-house, painting a beautiful waterfall." Crome was evidently very popular with them all, as Hannah enters in her diary, " *Patterdale, August 28th.—* . . . We were very sorry to part with John Crome." He returned to Norwich and left the Gurneys to continue their tour. In the next or following year he made a sketching tour down the valley of the Wye.

Crome was now firmly established as a drawing-master. He possessed a large circle of patrons and pupils, and had become the leading spirit in the small art world in the city. The Norwich Society of Artists, as already stated in the Introduction, was inaugurated in 1803, and the first of its exhibitions, under the title of "The Norwich Exhibition of Works of Living Artists," was held two years later. Crome contributed twenty-two works, chiefly views round the city, and some sketches which he had made during his trips to the Lake District and the Wye Valley. One of the former was a large oil painting, *A View of Carrow Abbey*, which was originally in the possession of Dr. Martineau of Bracondale, Norwich. It was again exhibited at the Loan Exhibition in Norwich after Crome's death in 1821, and at the International Exhibition of 1862. It is important on account of its being one of Crome's earliest known oil-paintings, and showing his style at that period. The remains of the ancient abbey rise up darkly against a luminous evening sky, with a pool and two figures in the foreground ; the whole treatment is subdued and severe. The picture is now in the possession of Mr. Russell J. Colman, at Crown Point, Norwich.

Amongst other painters who sent works to this first exhibition of The Norwich Society were Robert Dixon, Charles Hodgson, Robert Ladbrooke and John Thirtle. The remaining contributors were chiefly amateurs and pupils. The Society was evidently democratic, for the President, according to its rules, changed every year. Crome was doubtless the leading spirit; he appears to have held the office on numerous occasions and was President at the time of his death. He gave strong support to the Society during his life, and sent more than two hundred and fifty works to the Exhibitions. A list of them, compiled by Mr. John Wodderspoon, was given in "The Norwich Mercury" in 1858 and afterwards reprinted for private circulation. It is a valuable record, and by means of it, even though the titles have been changed, many of Crome's paintings have been traced, and the years in which they were produced have been identified ; but some of his best productions were never shown at these exhibitions.

In the year 1814, after the downfall of Buonaparte, many hundreds of Englishmen flocked to Paris especially to see the art treasures in the Louvre, the spoils which Napoleon had seized during his victorious campaigns. Crome took the opportunity of seeing these masterpieces, and in the autumn set out on his journey accompanied by two friends, J. Freeman and David Coppin. They crossed the Channel and set foot on the Continent. A description of his journey onwards and his arrival at the gay city is given in a letter written to his wife. It was printed in " The Eastern Daily Express." January 31, 1885, and reads as follows :

PARIS, *October* 10*th*, 1814.

MY DEAR WIFE—After one of the most pleasant journeys of one hundred and seventy miles over one of the most fertile countreys I ever saw we arrived in the capital of France. You may imagine how everything struck us with surprise ; people of all nations going to and fro— Turks, Jews, etc. I shall not enter into ye particulars in this my letter, but suffice it to say we are all in good health, and in good lodgings—that in

Paris is the one great difficulty. We have been at St. Cloud and Versailes ; I cannot describe it on letter. We have seen three palaces the most magnificent in world. I shall not trouble you with a long letter this time as the post goes out in an hour that time will not allow me was I so disposed. This morning I am going to see the object of my journey, that is the Thuilleries. I am told here I shall find many English artists. Glover has been painting. I believe he has not been copying, but looking, and painting one of his own compositions. Pray let me know how you are going on, giving best respects to all friends. I believe the English may boast of having the start of these foreigners, but a happier race of people there cannot be. I shall make this journey pay. I shall be very careful how I lay out my money. I have seen some shops. They ask treble what they will take, so you may suppose what a set they are. I shall see David tomorrow, and the rest of the artists when I can find time. I write this before I know what I am going about at ye Thuilleries as the post compels me.—I am, etc., yours till death, JOHN CROME.

The crowds of the gay city evidently attracted Crome, as he made a sketch of the Boulevard des Italiens with numerous figures. From it he painted the picture (Plate XIX) which he contributed to the Norwich Exhibition in the following year. He depicted the scene in brighter colours than was his wont. The same remark applies to the *Fishmarket on the Beach at Boulogne* (Plate XXIV), sketched on his return journey, but not produced as a large painting until 1820. Whilst on the Continent it is evident that he visited Ostend, as he made paintings from the neighbourhood of the town. He stated in his letter to his wife that he had a pleasant journey of one hundred and seventy miles to Paris, accordingly he may have landed at this port. Crome painted some evening effects, and *Bruges River, Ostend in the Distance* (Plate XVII), shown at the Norwich Exhibition in 1816, is a good representative work. *Moonlight on the Yare* (Plate VI) was exhibited two years earlier.

After this visit to Paris Crome does not appear to have made any other important tour. He preferred his home life, surrounded by his family. The natural scenery of Norfolk, for which he had so much affection, mainly inspired him. He painted, as he said, for " air and space," and took no poetic licence with his subjects; he simply represented Nature as he saw her. He was content to exhibit his paintings at Norwich, and only contributed thirteen pictures, between the years 1806 and 1818, to the Royal Academy. An important contribution was made to Somerset House in 1808, *Blacksmith's Shop, near Hingham* (Plate XXII). It was probably unsold and returned to Norwich, for this painting was lent to the Loan Exhibition after his death in 1821, by his son Frederick

Crome. In the catalogue of John Berney Crome's sale in 1834 is the following entry: "The Blacksmith's Shop by the late Mr. Crome, one of his best pictures in the style of Gainsborough"; it was sold for only six pounds. This painting and the *Woody Landscape at Colney* (Plate XXIII) are now in America. In his early works Crome was influenced, as already stated, by Wilson as well as by Gainsborough, and the *Landscape* (Plate II) may be quoted as an example.

Whilst visiting the country houses in his profession as a drawing-master, Crome must have seen many Dutch paintings, including works by Hobbema and Ruysdael. Through these he may be said to have been subconsciously influenced and to have acquired a taste for collecting old masters for himself, for he had almost a mania for attending sales at auction-rooms and buying bargains. He accumulated books, prints and drawings, and even went as far on one occasion as to purchase a cartload of headstones. The family eventually remonstrated and persuaded him to dispose of his collection. The following notice of the sale appeared in "The Norfolk Chronicle": "At Mr. Noverre's Rooms, Yarmouth, on Wednesday, the 23rd September, 1812, and two following days. A capital assemblage of Prints and Books of Prints; Etchings; Finished Drawings and Sketches by the best masters—Woollett, Strange, Fitler, Bartolozzi, Rembrandt, Waterloo, etc. They are the genuine sole property of Mr. Crome of Norwich—a great part of whose life has been spent in collecting them. Descriptive catalogues, price 6d. each, of the booksellers of Yarmouth, Norwich, Lynn, Ipswich, and Bury." As no auctioneer's name is mentioned, either in the advertisement or in the catalogue, it has been said that Crome acted as auctioneer himself. How the sale came to be held at Yarmouth is not clear. Allan Cunningham says that Mr. Dawson Turner, who lived there, suggested to Crome that he should have a sale of his works, but no picture by him appears in the catalogue. In spite of the dispersal of this collection, Crome continued to indulge in his hobby and gradually acquired a fresh one.

The Grove Scene, Marlingford (Plate VIII), which was sold at the Joseph Beecham sale in 1917 for five thousand three hundred guineas; the smaller *Mousehold Heath* (Plate IV), in the Victoria and Albert Museum; and the celebrated *Mousehold Heath* in the National Gallery, are of the same period, the two former being painted in 1815, and the last about 1816. In the foreground of all three pictures Crome has introduced carefully painted wild flowers and weeds. He made still-life studies of these plants, and in the Norwich Castle Museum is the *Study of a Burdock*, beautifully executed and relieved by a dark background. Mr. Arthur Michael Samuel, M.P., has in his possession a somewhat similar study entitled *The Water Vole*. The larger picture of *Mousehold Heath* was in

14

the possession of Messrs. Freeman of Norwich for many years. Failing to dispose of it, they had it cut into two pieces, with a view to being able to sell them separately, but without the desired result. Eventually the two portions were sold to Mr. Yetts, an auctioneer at Great Yarmouth, who had the painting restored, and afterwards lent it to the London International Exhibition of 1862, when it was acquired for the nation.

Crome was sufficiently prosperous to be enabled to keep two ponies in order to drive or ride to his numerous pupils' homes. He used to go as far as Yarmouth to see his friend Dawson Turner. The sea itself appears to have had no attractions for him, but he produced several beach scenes and views of shipping of which *Yarmouth Harbour* (Plate XVIII), and *Yarmouth Jetty* (Plate XXI) are good examples.

As *Mousehold Heath* may be said to be Crome's largest painting "for air and space," similarly *The Poringland Oak*, also in the National Gallery, may be stated to be his finest painting of a tree. Three of the four boys bathing in a pool in the foreground represent Crome's sons, and the fourth is his nephew, John Berney Ladbrooke. The figures were worked upon by Crome's friend Michael Sharp. The youngest son, Michael Sharp Crome, was born in 1813, and as he is shown as a lad of about five years of age, it may be fairly assumed the picture was executed in 1818. Another fine example and worthy to rank with *The Poringland Oak*, although smaller in size, is *Woody Landscape at Colney* (Plate XXIII); it was executed eight years earlier and was sent to the exhibition of the Norwich Society in 1810.

Crome painted in water-colours, but none of his drawings have any importance in relation to his oil-paintings. They were mostly done in slight washes, and chiefly executed as examples for his pupils. In the production of *Woodland Scene, Dunham, Norfolk* (Plate XXXI), Crome has carried his work further and made a charming finished drawing. Like most of the painters of the Norwich School, Crome produced some etchings. These were done between the years 1809 and 1813. He does not appear to have been satisfied with them, for although he published a prospectus in 1812 with a view to issuing them to the public, and obtained a list of subscribers, the matter was never carried any further by him. He etched both on soft and on hard ground, but his plates were unevenly bitten. In 1834 a series of thirty-one of these etchings was brought out under the title of "Norfolk Picturesque Scenery." Four years later seventeen of them were re-issued and called "Etchings of Views of Norfolk by the late John Crome." The plates, however, had become worn and the beautiful *Mousehold Heath* was ruined by ruled lines across the magnificent sky. The issue is only valuable for the memoir of Crome written by Dawson Turner.

The genial character of Crome endeared him to every one with whom he came in contact. Dawson Turner wrote: "I had the greatest regard for him when living. I enjoyed his Society: I admired his talents: I valued the man and I highly appreciated the good sense which led him to confine himself exclusively to the representation of nature, and to be satisfied with her as she offered herself to his eyes." It has also been said of him "as his sphere of operations enlarged his talents as an artist were acknowledged, and his manners as a man universally gained him friends. He was equally at home and equally welcome at the tables of the rich and high-born as at those of a station similar to his own."

Crome was not destined to live to an old age. In April, 1821, he had determined to paint a large picture of a "water frolic"—an East Anglian term for a regatta, now almost disused—at Wroxham, but he was suddenly taken ill and died on the 22nd of the month. To the very last Crome's thoughts were directed towards the art to which he was so devoted. It is said that on the day of his death he begged his eldest son never to forget the dignity of Art. "John, my boy," he exclaimed, "paint, but paint for fame, and if your subject is only a pigsty—dignify it." Just before passing away he suddenly cried out "Oh Hobbema! my dear Hobbema, how I loved you!" He was buried in St. George's-at-Colegate, with a great demonstration of affection and respect. According to "The Norwich Mercury" "Mr. Sharp and Mr. Vincent came from town on purpose, and Mr. Stark was also present. An immense concourse of people bore grateful testimony to the estimation in which his character was generally held."

Crome had continued to collect pictures, prints and books up to the last, and after his death a five days' sale took place, in the Norwich Society's room at Sir Benjamin Wrench's Court, of the vast store he had accumulated. None of his own work was included in the sale. In November of the same year the Norwich Society of Artists held a loan exhibition of Crome's pictures in their own rooms. More than one hundred works were lent by their owners, and the catalogue of the Exhibition forms a valuable record of many of "Old" Crome's authentic paintings, for few of them, at that date, had gone further afield than Norwich and the country seats in its neighbourhood.

PLATE I

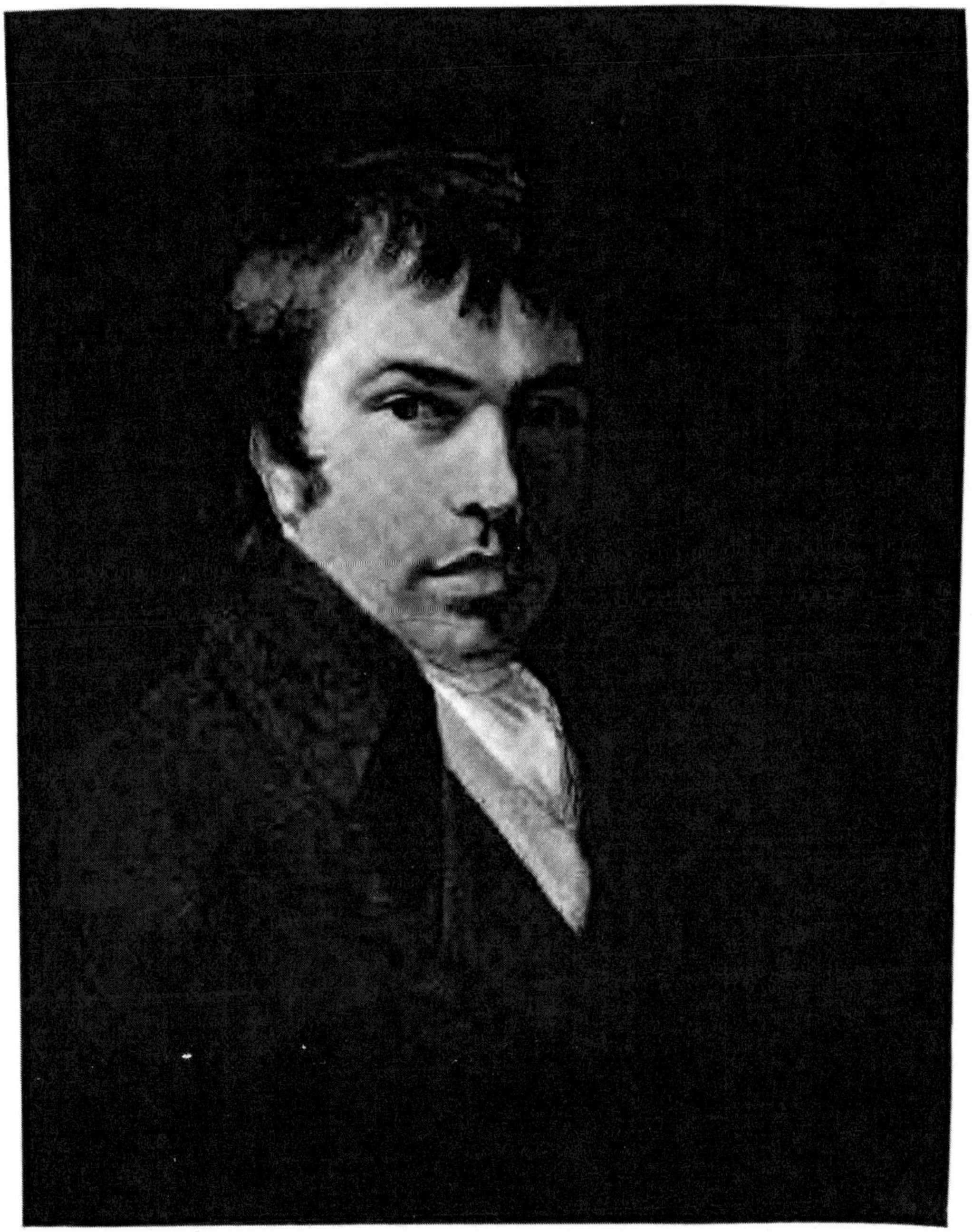

(From the portrait in the Castle Museum, Norwich. Colman Bequest)

JOHN CROME. BY JOHN OPIE, R.A.

PLATE II

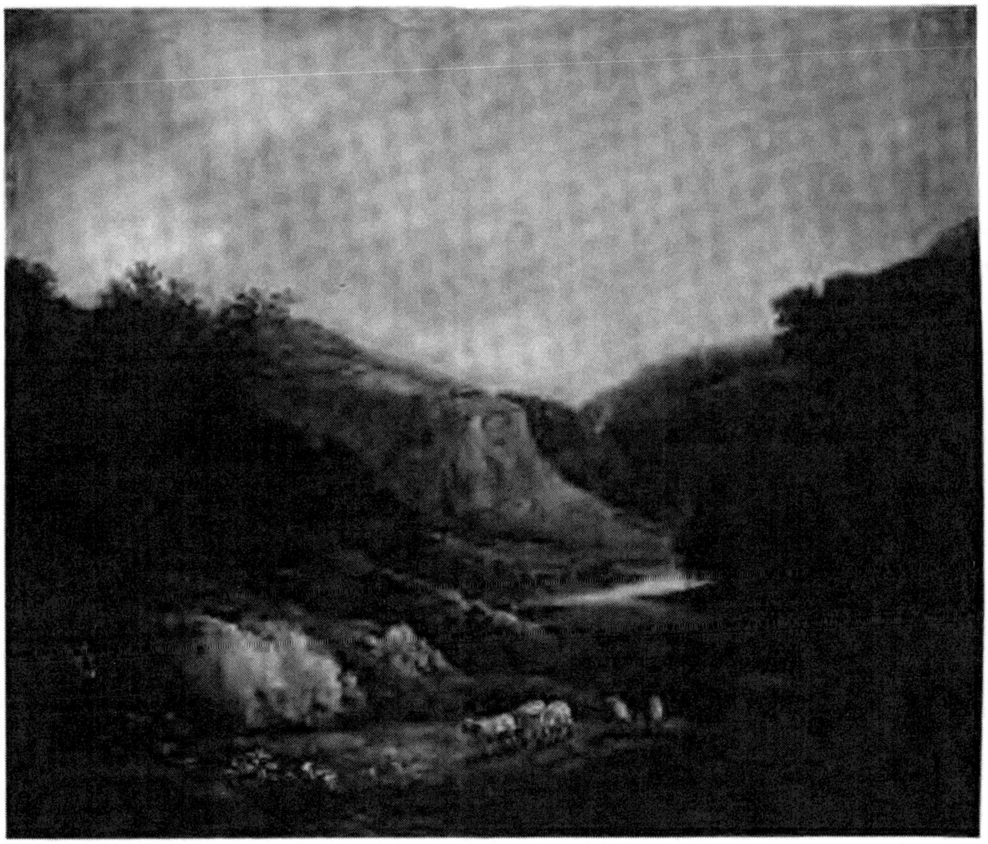

(In the possession of Colonel Sir George Lindsay Holford, K.C.V.O.)

LANDSCAPE. OIL PAINTING BY JOHN CROME (36 × 28 INCHES)

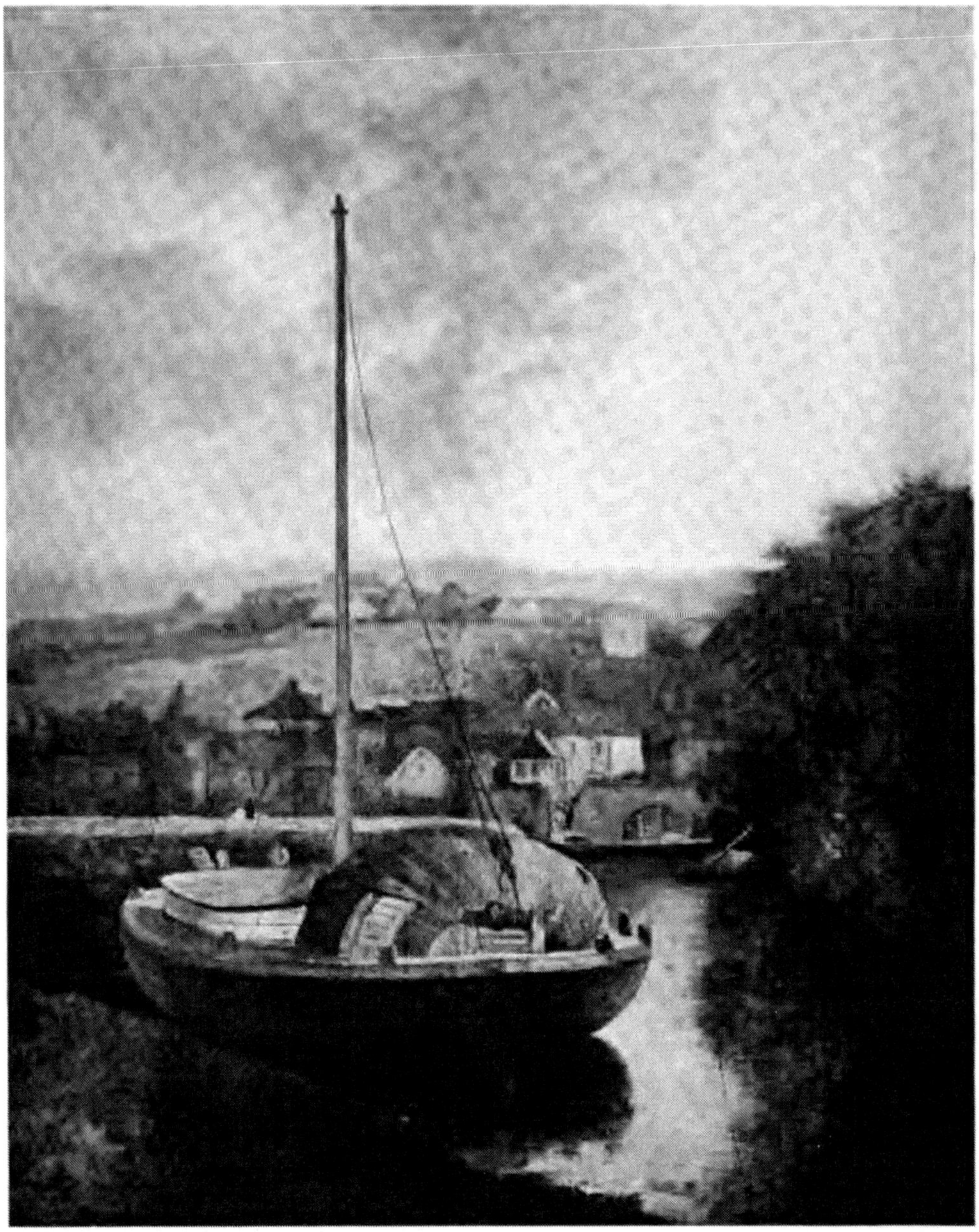

(In the Castle Museum, Norwich)

"VIEW ON THE WENSUM." OIL PAINTING BY JOHN CROME (16½ × 20 INCHES)

PLATE IV

"MOUSEHOLD HEATH, NEAR NORWICH." OIL PAINTING BY JOHN CROME (32 × 21½ INCHES)

(In the Victoria and Albert Museum, London)

PLATE V

(In the possession of Mrs. Louis Raphael)

"THE RETURN OF THE FLOCK—EVENING." OIL PAINTING BY JOHN CROME (24 × 18 INCHES)

PLATE VI

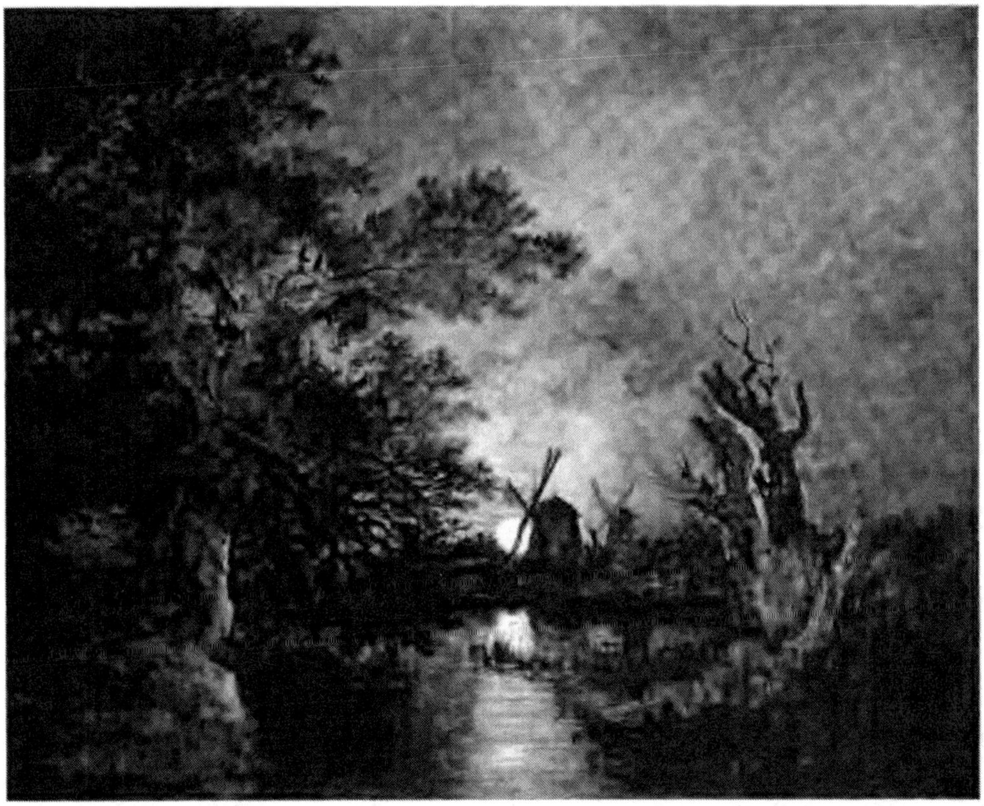

(*In the possession of H. Darell-Brown, Esq.*)

"MOONLIGHT ON THE YARE." OIL PAINTING BY JOHN CROME (48×37½ INCHES)

PLATE VII

"LANDSCAPE: GROVE SCENE." OIL PAINTING BY JOHN CROME (25½ × 18½ INCHES)

(In the possession of Russell J. Colman, Esq.)

PLATE VIII

"THE GROVE SCENE, MARLINGFORD." OIL
PAINTING BY JOHN CROME (38½ × 53½ INCHES)

PLATE IX

"THE VILLAGE GLADE." OIL PAINT-
ING BY JOHN CROME (36 × 44 INCHES)

PLATE X

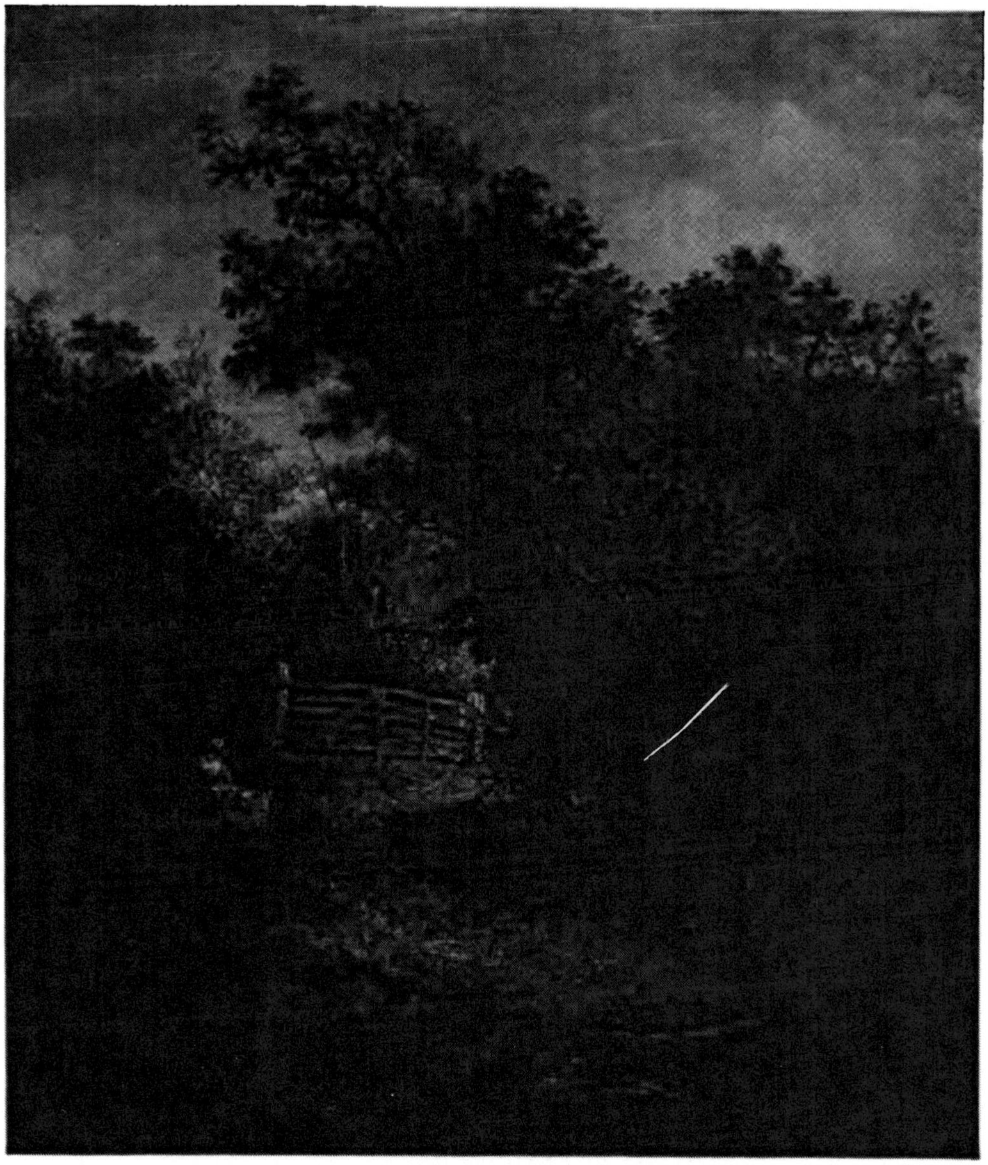

(*In the possession of Russell J. Colman, Esq.*)

"THE GATE." OIL PAINTING BY JOHN CROME (24½ × 27 INCHES)

PLATE XI

(In the Castle Museum, Norwich. Colman Bequest)

"BACK OF THE NEW MILLS, NORWICH." OIL PAINTING BY JOHN CROME (21 × 16 INCHES)

PLATE XII

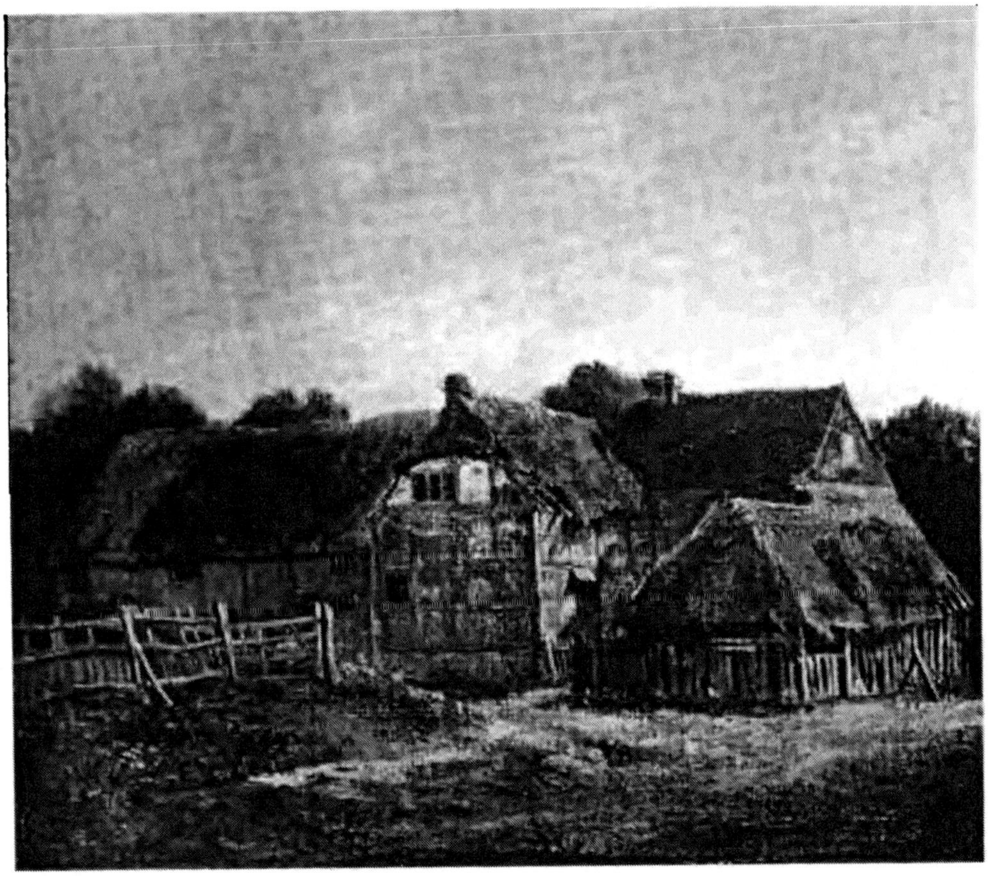

*(In the possession of
Arthur Michael Samuel, Esq., M.P.)*

"COTTAGE NEAR LAKENHAM." OIL PAINTING BY JOHN CROME (13 × 11 INCHES)

PLATE XIII

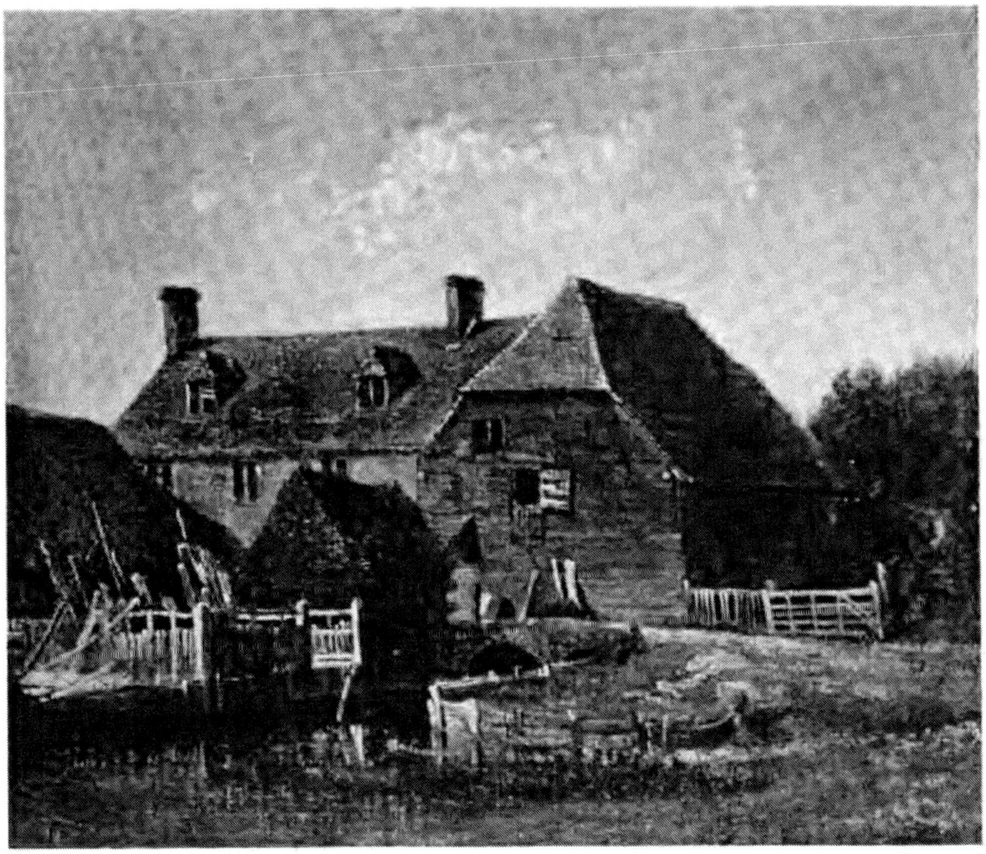

(In the possession of Arthur Michael Samuel, Esq., M.P.)

"MILL NEAR LAKENHAM." OIL PAINTING BY JOHN CROME (13×11 INCHES)

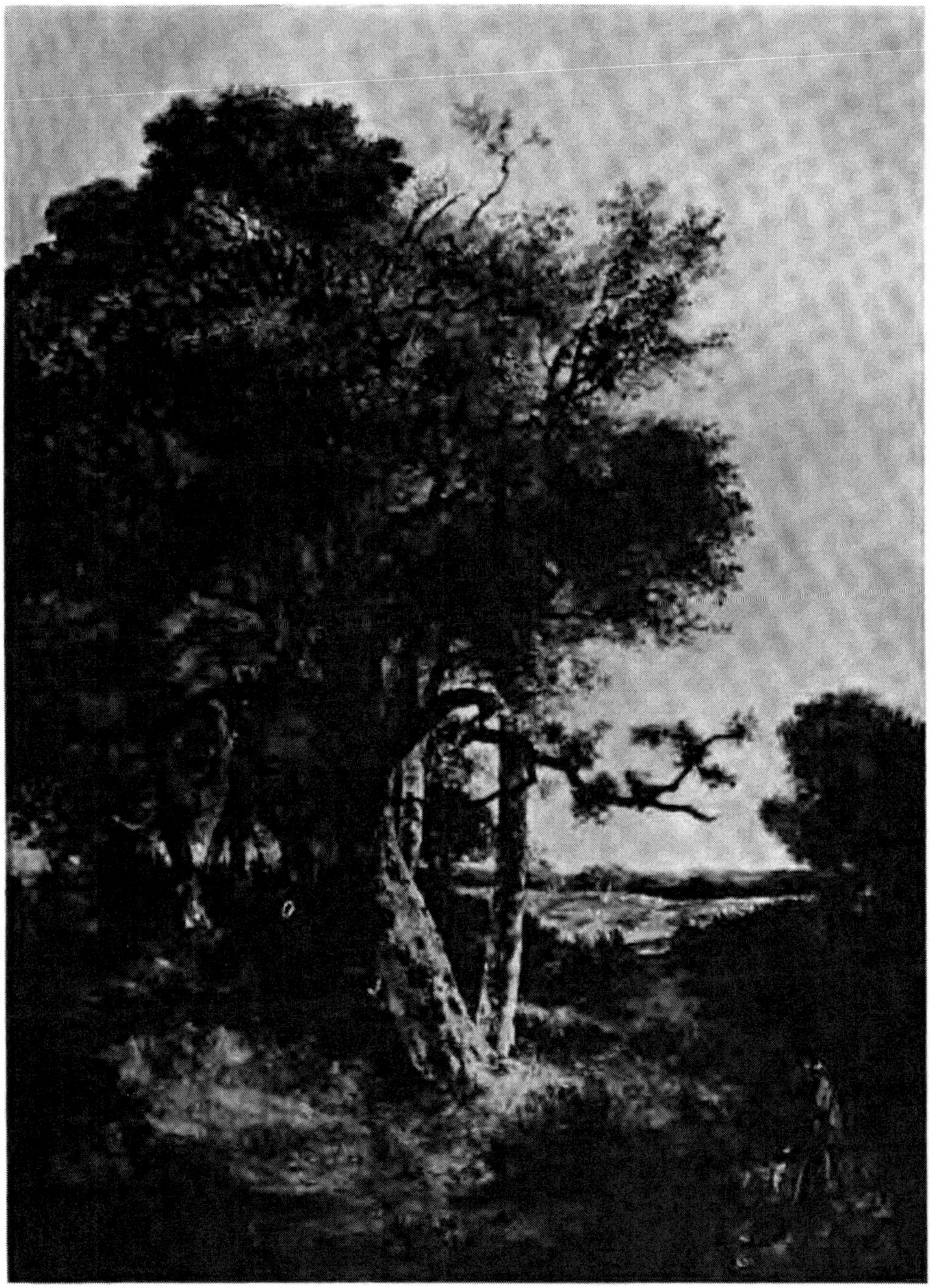

(In the Victoria and Albert Museum, London)

"ON THE SKIRTS OF THE FOREST." OIL PAINTING BY JOHN CROME (30½ × 42 INCHES)

PLATE XV

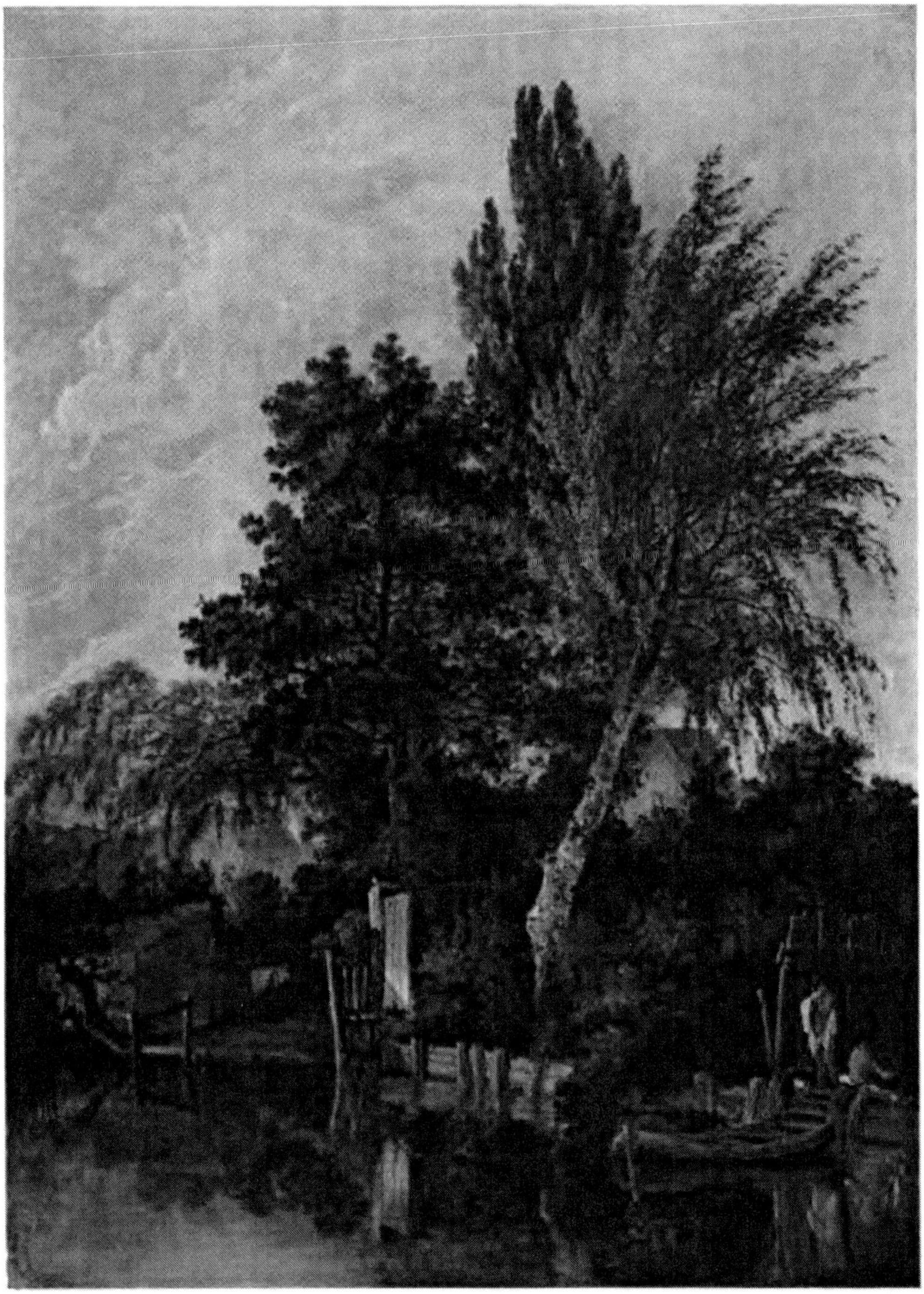

(In the possession of
H. Darell-Brown, Esq.)

"A BATHING SCENE—VIEW ON THE WENSUM AT THORPE, NORWICH." OIL PAINTING BY JOHN CROME (13¾ × 18½ INCHES)

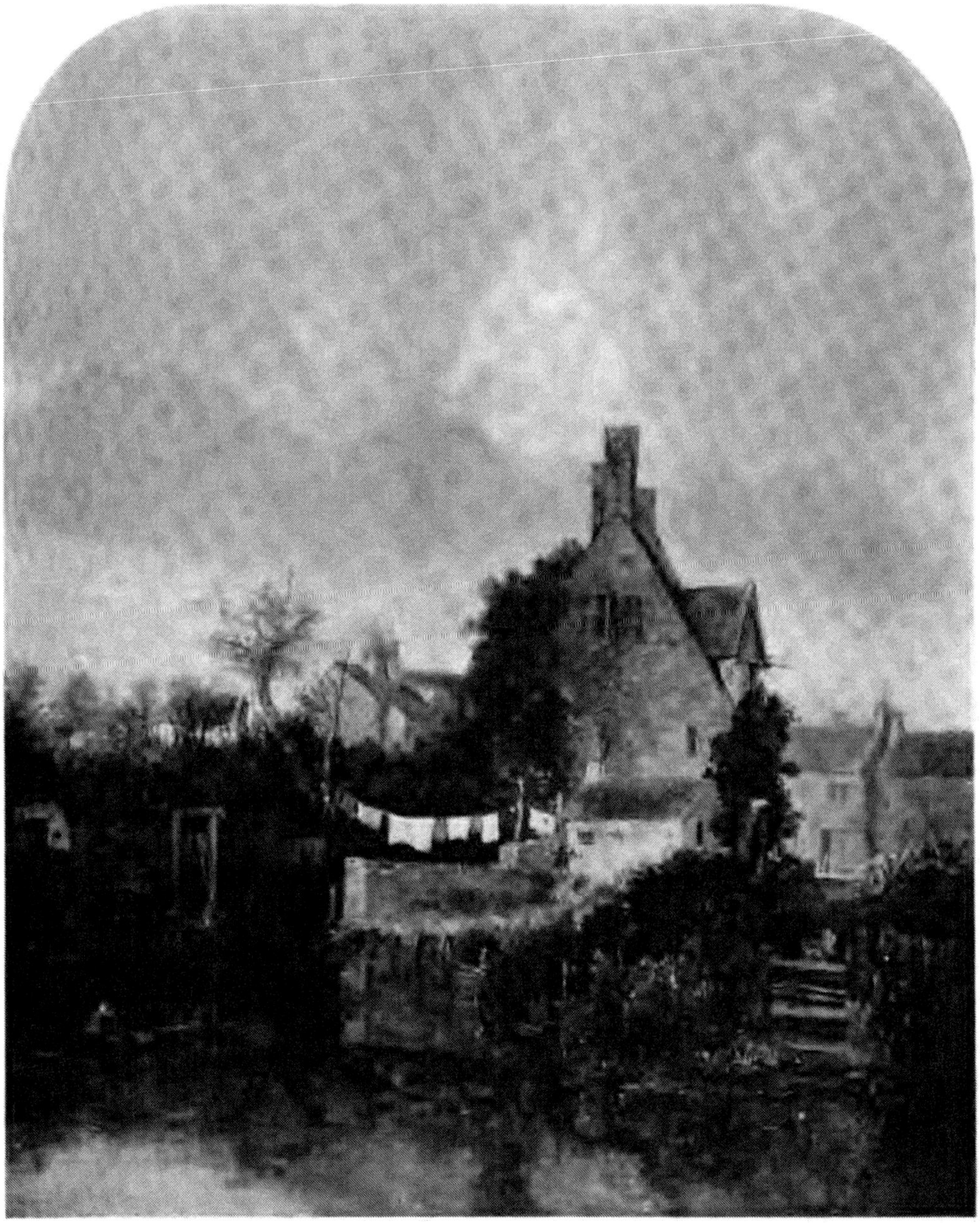

(Formerly in the possession of Mrs. T. Temple Silver)

"BACK RIVER, NORWICH." OIL PAINTING BY JOHN CROME (16 × 19½ INCHES)

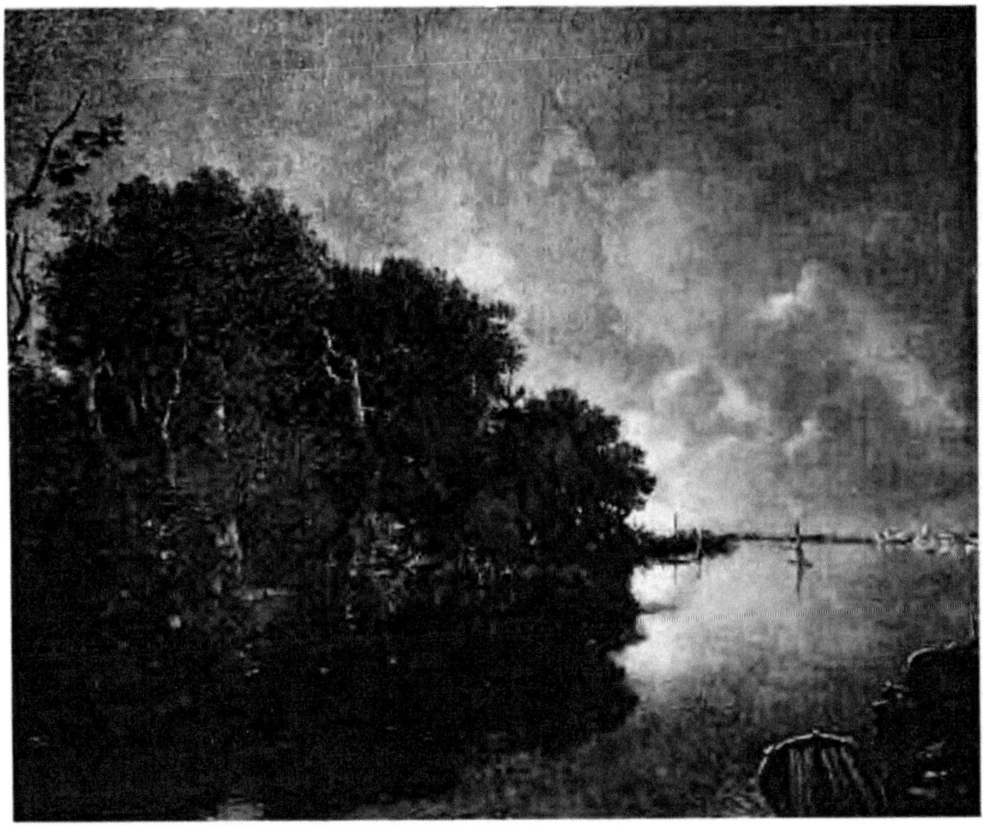

(In the Castle Museum, Norwich
Colman Bequest)

"BRUGES RIVER, OSTEND IN THE DISTANCE; MOONLIGHT." OIL PAINTING BY JOHN CROME (31¾ × 25¼ INCHES)

PLATE XVIII

"YARMOUTH HARBOUR." OIL PAINTING BY JOHN CROME (25¼ × 15¼ INCHES)

(In the possession of H. Darell-Brown, Esq.)

PLATE XIX

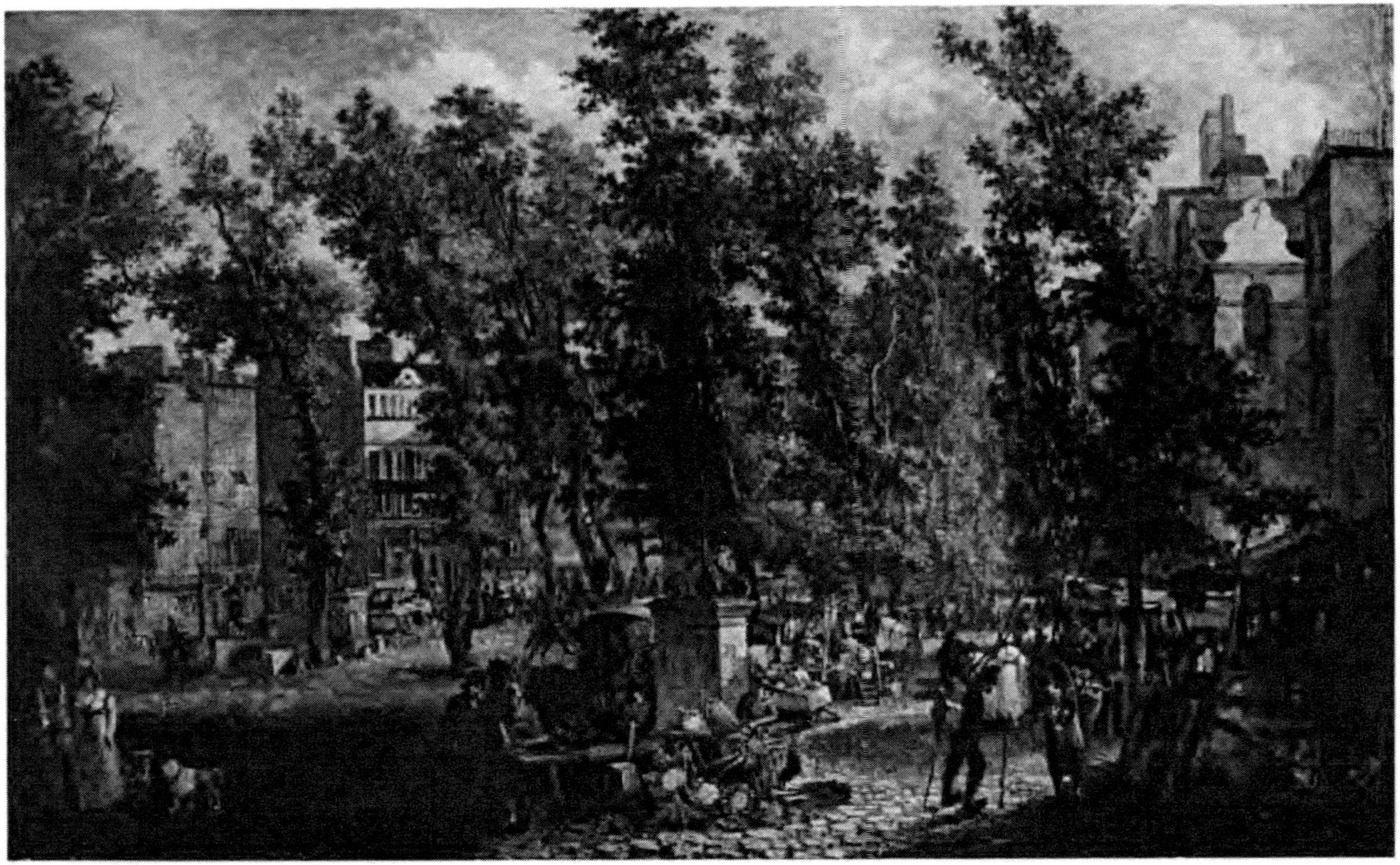

(In the possession of J. H. Gurney, Esq.)

"BOULEVARD DES ITALIENS, PARIS, 1814." OIL PAINTING BY JOHN CROME (33½ × 21½ INCHES)

PLATE XX

(In the possession of Russell J. Colman, Esq.)

"ROAD WITH POLLARDS." OIL PAINTING BY JOHN CROME (42 × 28 INCHES)

PLATE XXI

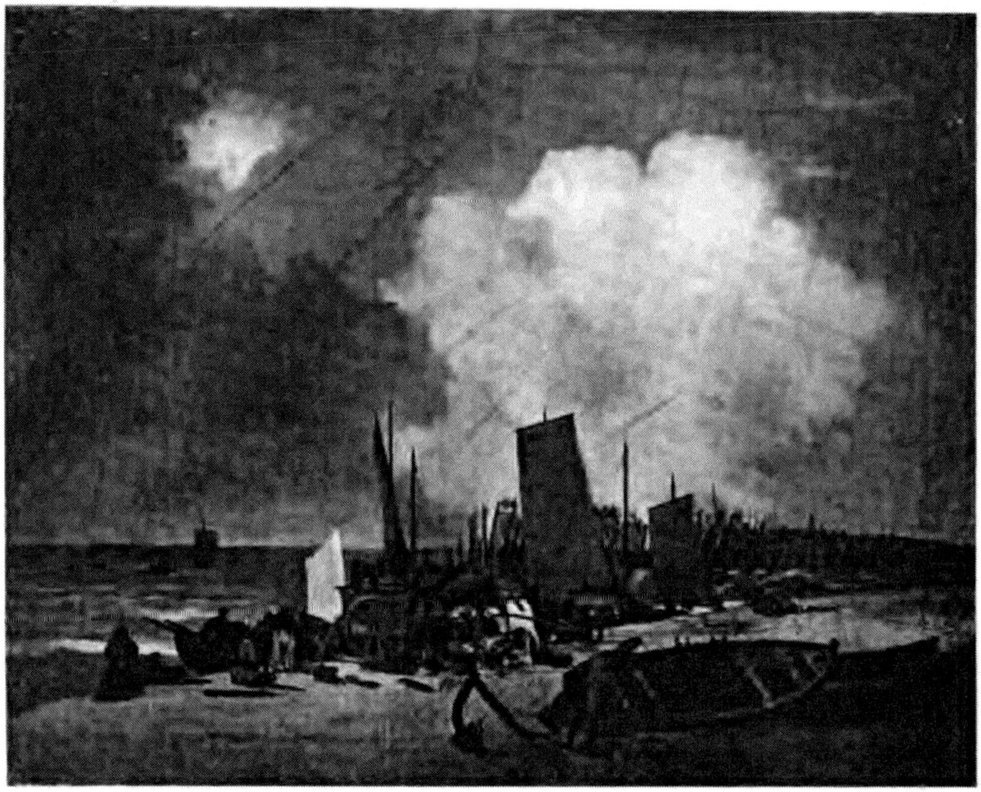

(In the Castle Museum, Norwich
Colman Bequest)

"YARMOUTH JETTY." OIL PAINTING
BY JOHN CROME (22½ × 17½ INCHES)

PLATE XXII

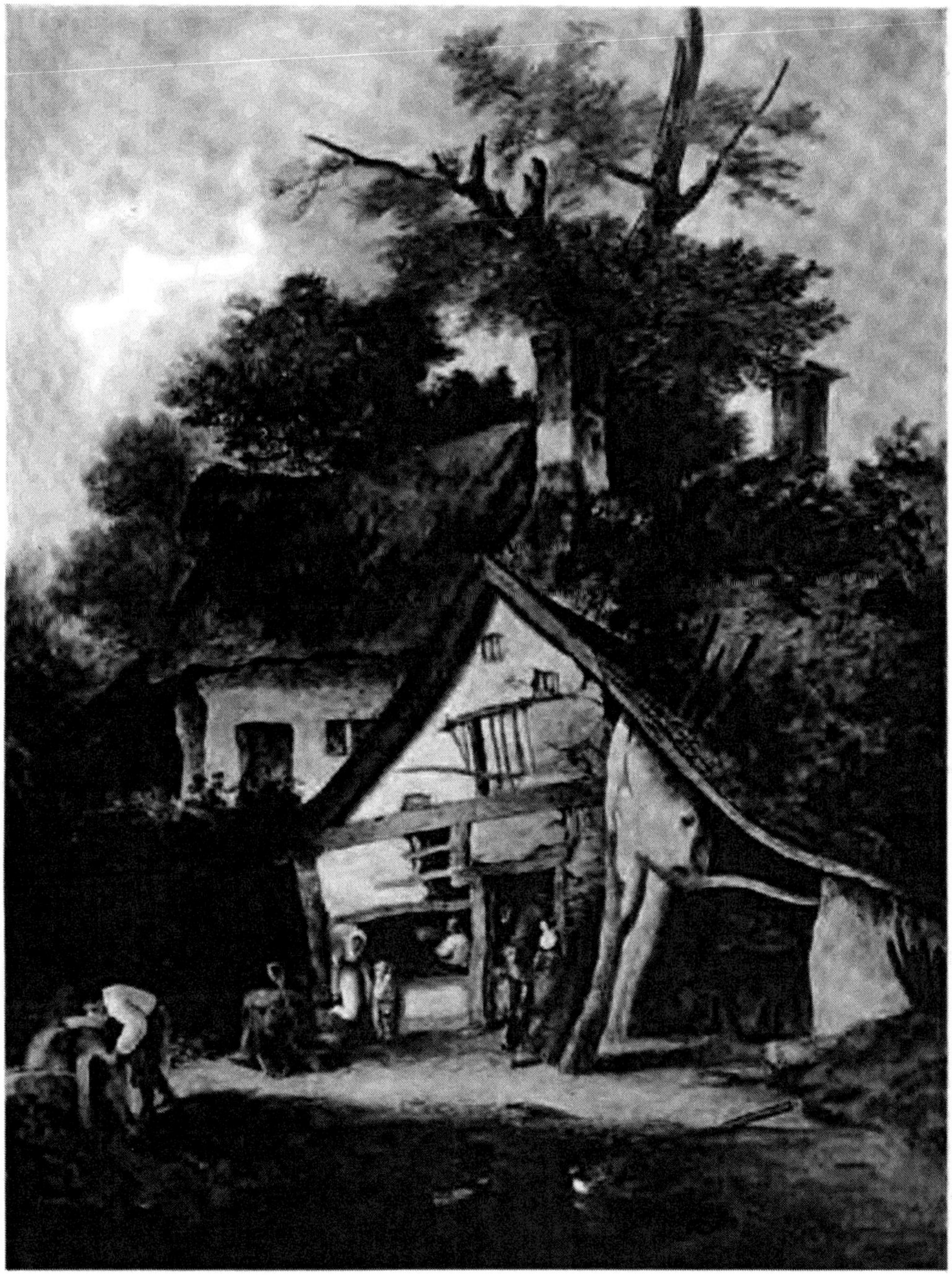

(In the possession of John H. McFadden, Esq.)

"BLACKSMITH'S SHOP, NEAR HINGHAM, NORFOLK." OIL PAINTING BY JOHN CROME (45 × 58 INCHES)

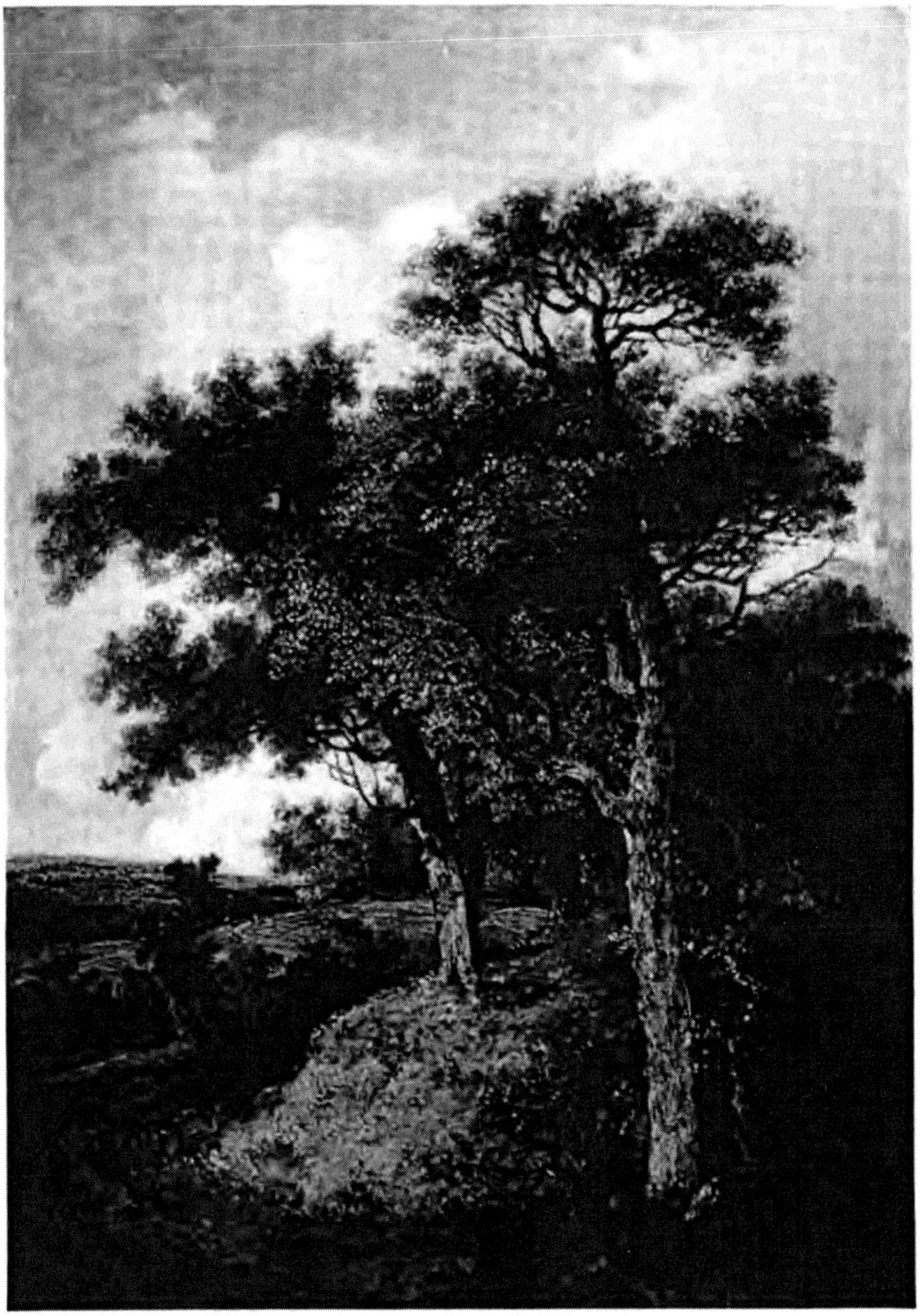

(In the possession of John H. McFadden, Esq.)

"WOODY LANDSCAPE AT COLNEY." OIL PAINTING BY JOHN CROME (16½ × 22 INCHES)

PLATE XXIV

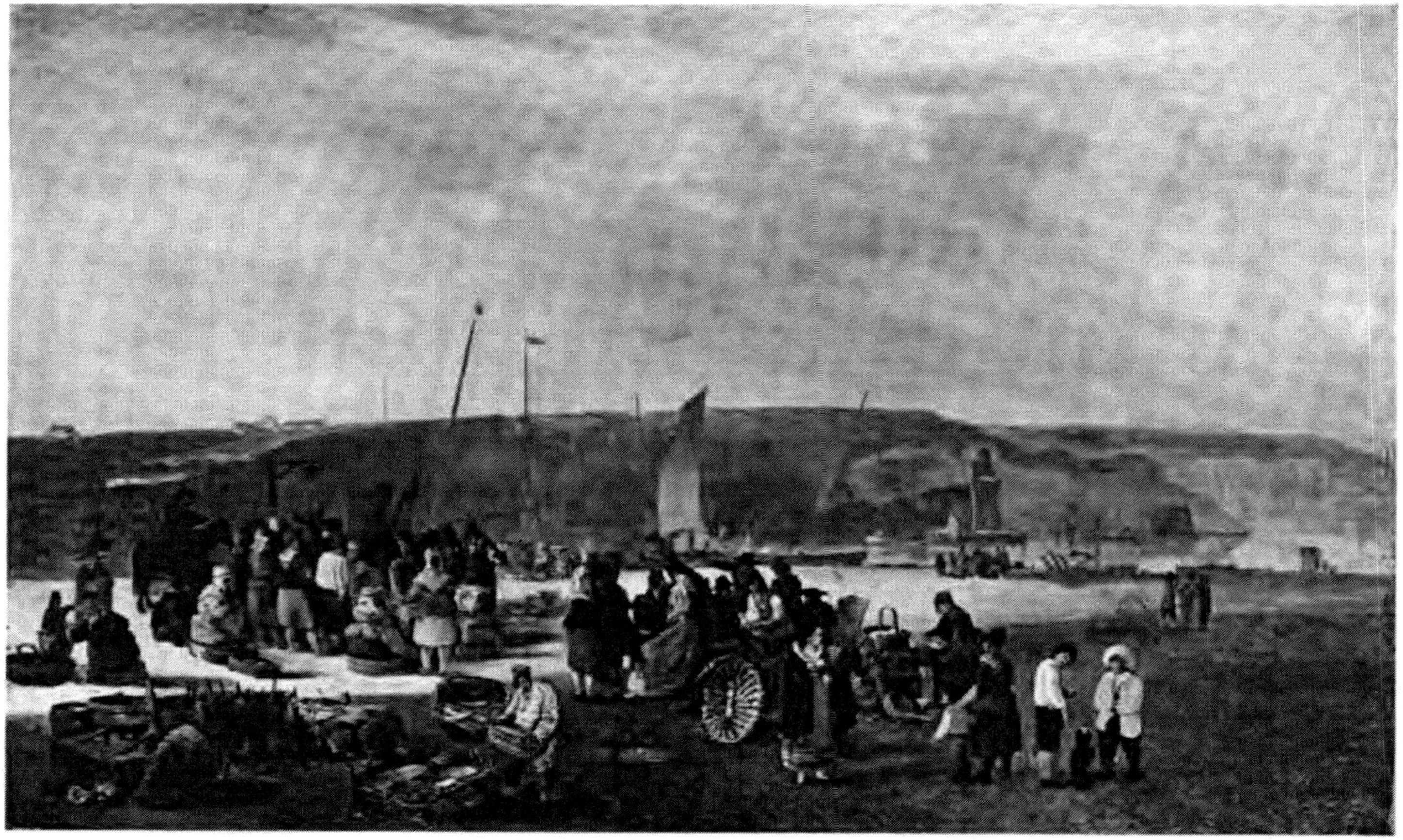

(*In the possession of J. H. Gurney, Esq.*)

"FISHMARKET ON THE BEACH AT BOULOGNE." OIL PAINTING BY JOHN CROME (33¾ × 21¾ INCHES)

PLATE XXV

(*In the possession of Russell J. Colman, Esq.*)

"THATCHED BUILDINGS." WATER-COLOUR BY JOHN CROME (14¼ × 10 INCHES)

PLATE XXVI

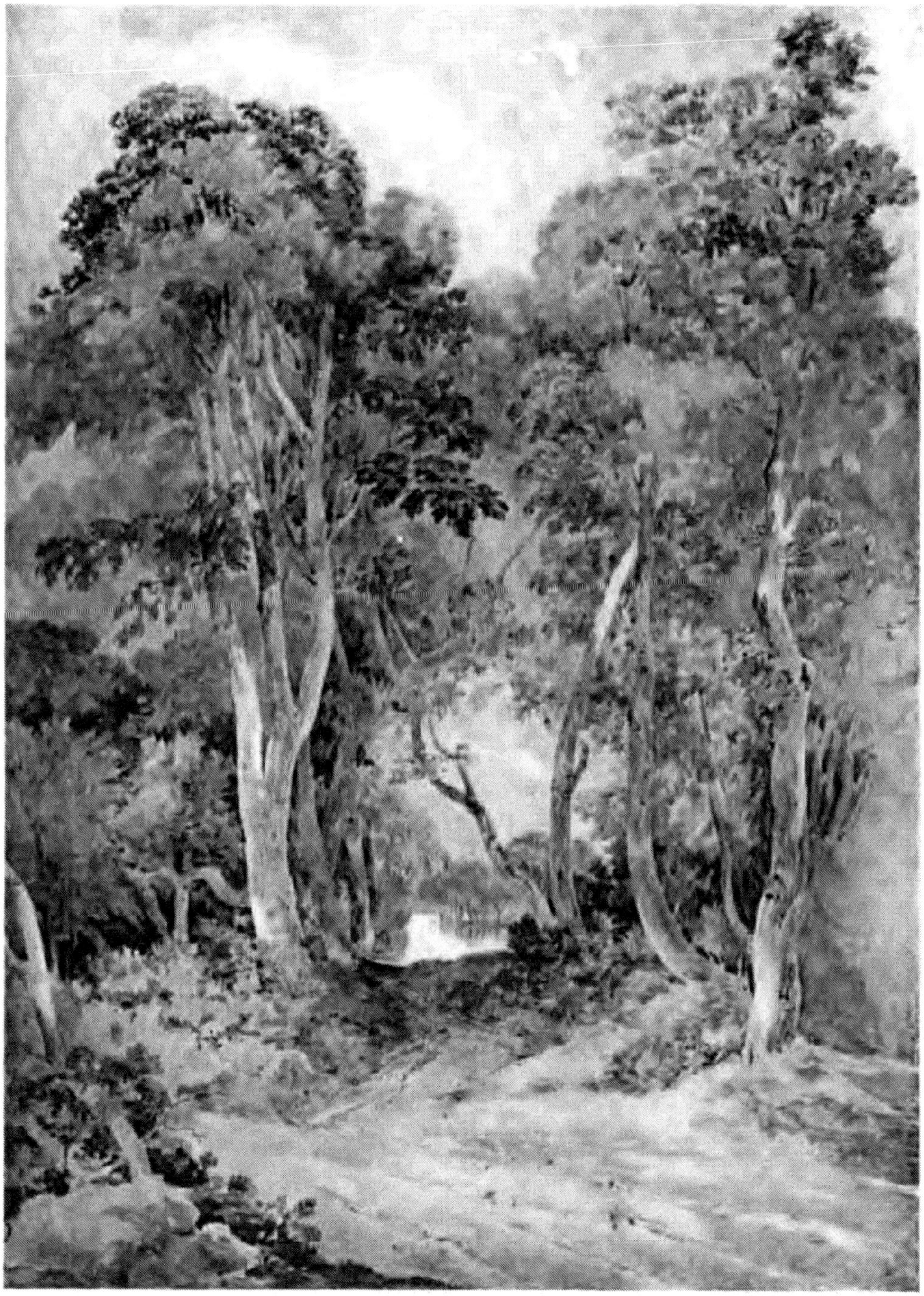

(In the possession of Russell J. Colman, Esq.)

"LANE SCENE NEAR NORWICH." WATER-COLOUR BY JOHN CROME (16¾ × 22¼ INCHES)

PLATE XXVII

"LANDSCAPE NEAR LAKENHAM." WATER-COLOUR BY JOHN CROME (10½ × 6 INCHES)

(In the possession of Russell J. Colman, Esq.)

PLATE XXVIII

"MALTINGS ON THE WENSUM." WATER-COLOUR BY JOHN CROME (17¾ × 10½ INCHES)

(In the possession of Russell J. Colman, Esq.)

PLATE XXIX

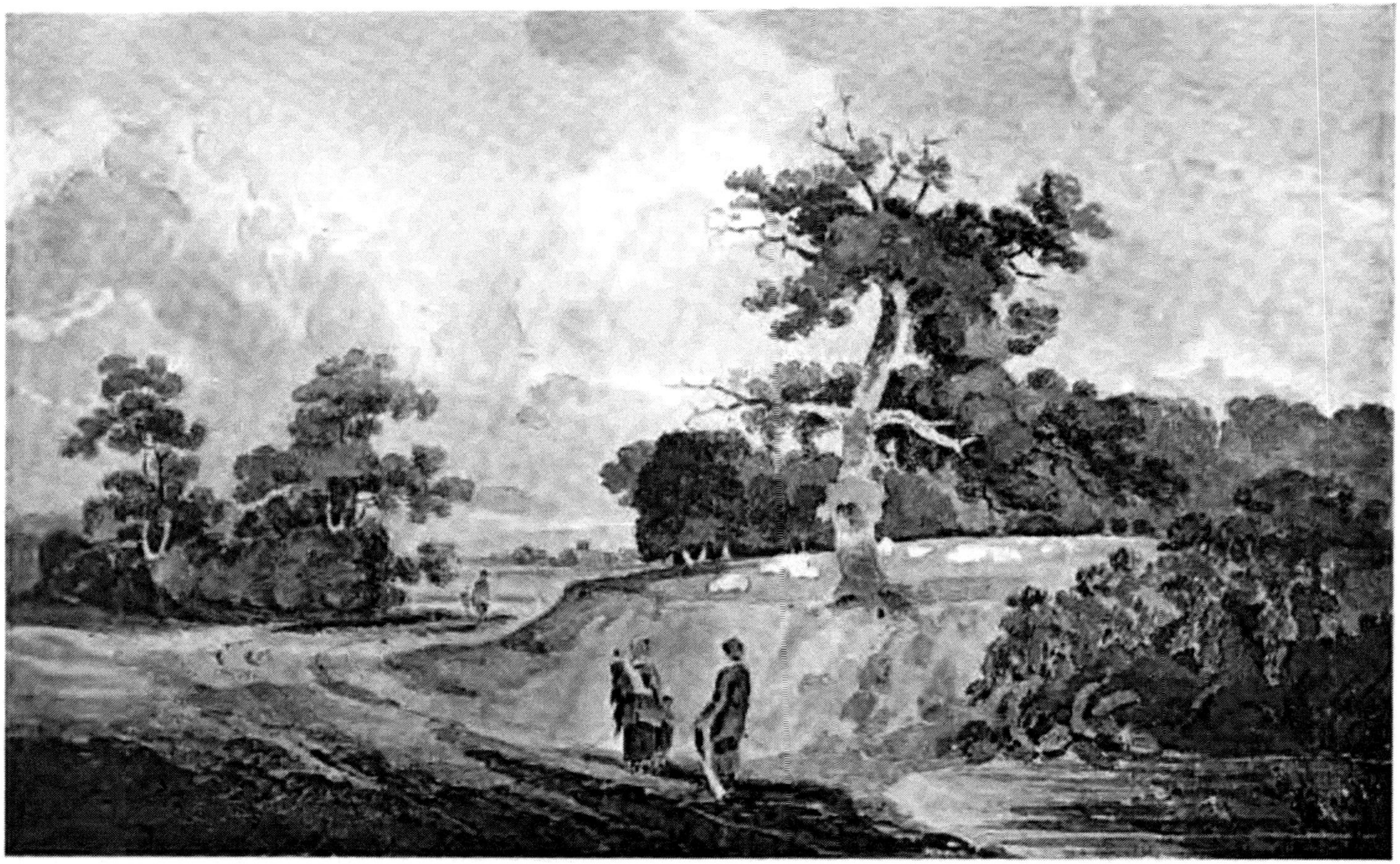

(In the British Museum, London)

"LANDSCAPE WITH FIGURES." WATER-COLOUR BY JOHN CROME ($12\frac{3}{8} \times 7\frac{7}{8}$ INCHES)

PLATE XXX

"WAITING FOR THE FERRY." WATER-COLOUR BY JOHN CROME (12¾ × 7¾ INCHES)

(In the British Museum, London)

PLATE XXXI

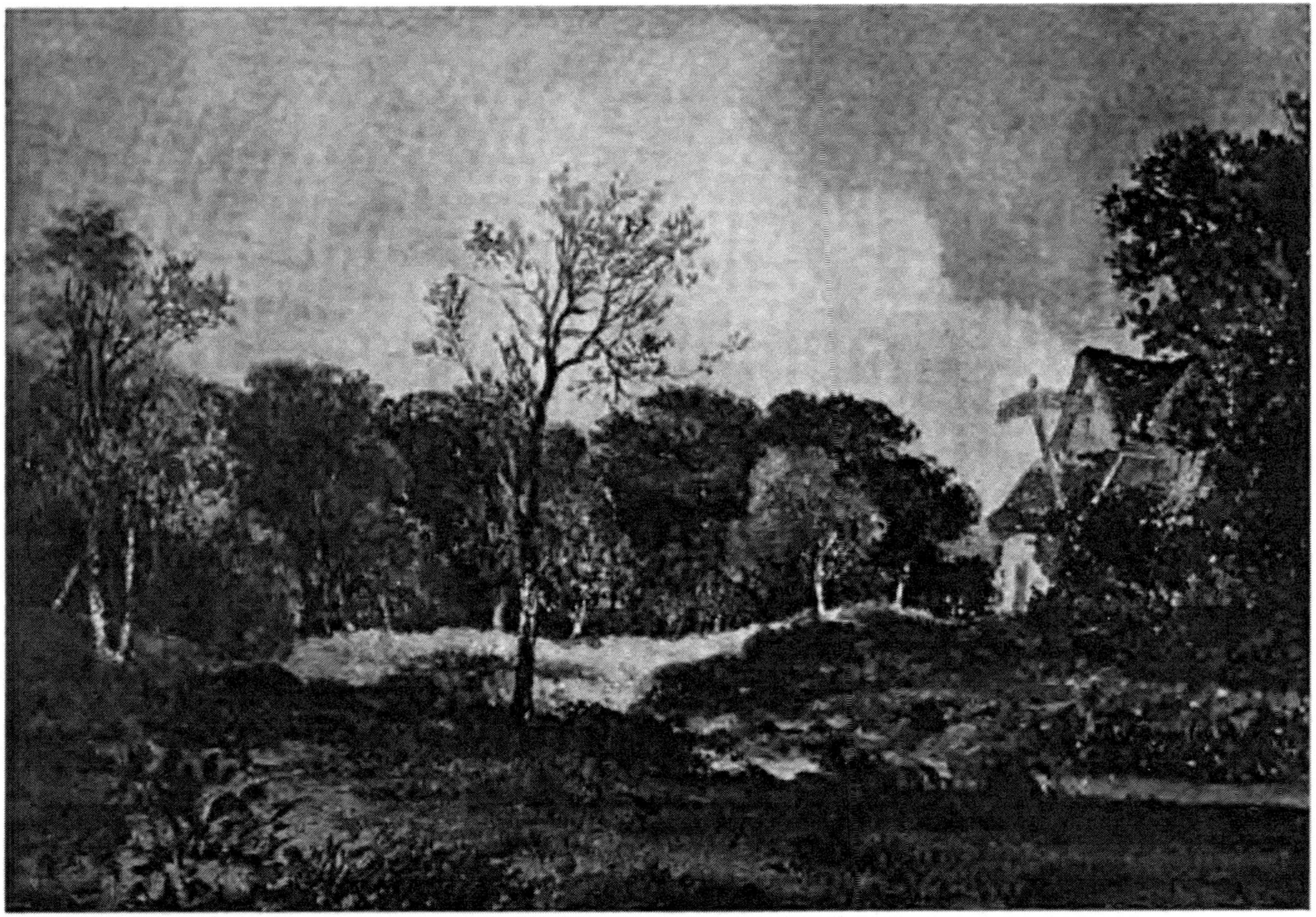

(In the British Museum, London)

"WOODLAND SCENE, DUNHAM, NORFOLK." WATER-COLOUR BY JOHN CROME ($9\frac{1}{4} \times 6\frac{3}{4}$ INCHES)

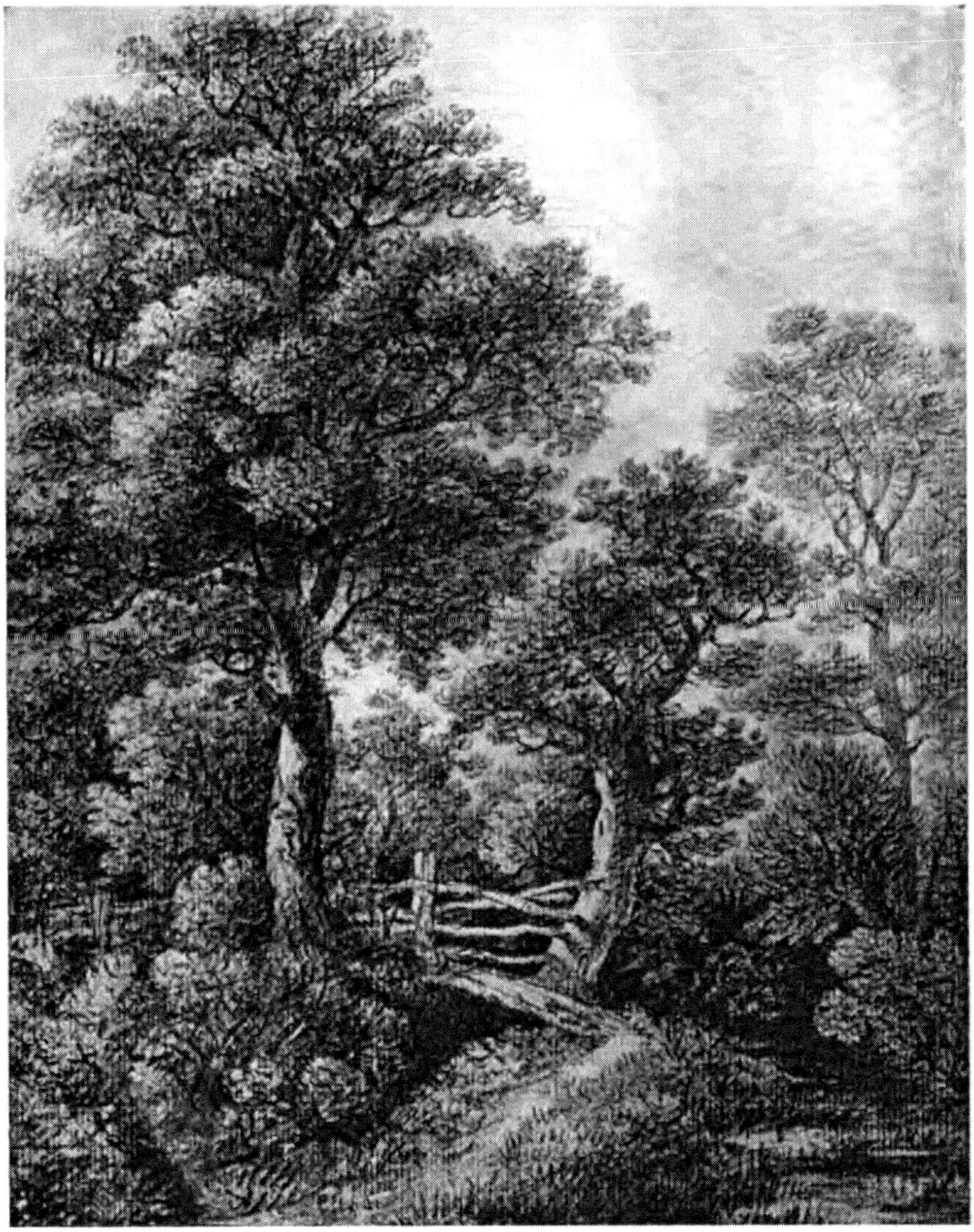

(In the possession of
Arthur Michael Samuel, Esq., M.P.)

PENCIL STUDY BY JOHN CROME (7 × 8¾ INCHES)

JOHN SELL COTMAN

IN the introduction to the catalogue of the Exhibition of the Society of Painters in Water-Colours held at the Egyptian Hall in 1821, the year previous to its removal to the premises in Pall Mall East which have ever since been the permanent home of the Society, it is stated that "Painting in Water-Colours may justly be regarded as a new art, and in its present application the invention of British artists; considerations which ought to have some influence on its public estimation and encouragement. Within a few years the materials employed in this species of painting, and the manner of using them, have been equally improved by new chemical discoveries and successful innovations on the old methods of practice. The feeble-tinted drawings, formerly supposed to be the utmost efforts of this art, have been succeeded by pictures not inferior in power to oil paintings, and equal in delicacy of tint and purity and airiness of tone." Twenty years previously Girtin and Turner had laid aside the "feeble-tinted drawings" and sought to impart to their paintings the luminosity and true colours of nature with perfect clearness and transparency; and John Sell Cotman had followed in their footsteps, but in a style peculiarly his own of flat broad washes with little attempt at relief or shadow. Edmund Cotman was a well-to-do draper and silk mercer in Cockey Lane—afterwards named Little London Street—Norwich; his eldest son, John Sell, was born on May 16, 1782, and educated at the Grammar School, in the Cathedral Close, when Dr. Forster, who became the first Vice-President of the Norwich Society of Artists, was headmaster. It was the father's intention that his son should join him in his business, but the boy had already shown signs of a desire to become a painter, and was accustomed to wander away into the country to make sketches of ruins and churches in the villages. The city, with its fine architecture and the surrounding neighbourhood, always had a fascination for him. Years afterwards he spoke of it as being "not to be equalled in its quiet way by any city in the British Empire, and beloved by me." In the Reeve Collection at the British Museum is a small drawing in india-ink of *Old Houses in Mill Lane, Newmarket Road, Norwich.** At the back of it is written by J. J. Cotman "J. S. C., drawn 1794," to which Mr. Reeve has added "John considered this the earliest drawing of his father's—I had it from Mr. Samuel, of Norwich." It is a remarkable drawing for a boy in his thirteenth year. Recognizing his son's disinclination for a commercial life the father sought the advice of John Opie, who replied, "let him rather black boots than follow the profession of

* Mill Lane is now called Brunswick Road, and this drawing has a special interest for the writer, as his grandfather was living in Norwich when Crome and Cotman were working there, and died in 1875 at Brunswick Road in his 95th year.

17

an artist." The boy was not to be deterred, however, and it was finally agreed that he should follow the profession of a painter.

According to Miss Turner, a daughter of Dawson Turner, "Cotman, giving up the idea of becoming a draper, came to London in 1798–9." Nothing is known of his early movements in the metropolis, but he did not waste his time, as almost immediately after his arrival he was awarded a "larger silver palette" by the Society of Arts, in 1809, for a drawing which had been submitted. In "Thaddeus of Warsaw," by Miss Jane Porter, the hero, a Polish noble named Zobieski, reduced to want, finds "his sole dependence must rest on his talents for painting. His taste easily perceived that there were many drawings exhibited for sale much inferior to those which he had executed for mere amusement." Accordingly, he attempts to sell his drawings to a printseller in Great Newport Street, but they are declined. Eventually the dealer agrees to accept six drawings a week for a guinea. It has been suggested that the incident was based upon what actually happened to young Cotman. This may have been true, as Miss Porter was sister to Sir Robert Ker Porter, and through her brother probably became acquainted with Cotman. That he did sell his drawings to print dealers is known, as John Thirtle, afterwards his brother-in-law, was in the habit, when coming to London, of looking into Ackerman's window to see if there were any new works by his brother artist. It is certain, however, that Cotman was not without means, as at first he lived in Gerrard Street, Soho, and afterwards in New Bond Street. He came under the patronage of Dr. Munro, and at his house on Adelphi Terrace, where his protogés assembled to copy drawings, Cotman probably first met Girtin and Turner. Girtin assisted in starting a club for practising landscape painting. The members met in the evening at each other's houses by rotation; a subject was chosen, and each treated it according to his own idea. The sketches became the property of the member at whose house they met. It is said that for this reason Turner declined to be one of the party. On the back of a moonlight composition by Louis Francia, in the Victoria and Albert Museum, is the following inscription:

"This drawing was made on Monday, May the 20th, 1799, at the room of Robert Ker Porter of No. 16 Great Newport Street, Leicester Square, in the very painting room that formerly was Sir Josuah (sic) Reynolds's, and since has been Dr. Samuel Johnson's; and for the first time on the above day convened a small and select Society of Young Painters under the title (as I give it) of the Brothers; met for the purpose of establishing by practice a school of Historic Landscape, the subjects being designs from poetick passages; L'. Francia. The Society consists of Worthington, J. C'. Denham, Treas', R'.

18

K^r. Porter, T^s. Girtin, **T^s.** Underwood, G^e. Samuel, and L^s. Francia, Secret^y."

Cotman joined the Society later, for there exists a drawing made at a meeting of the Club in May 1802, the subject being two lines of Cunningham. It bears the following inscription : "Cotman President, Present Alexander, Varley, Underwood, P. S. Munn, and visitor Wm. Munn." There had evidently been many changes in the membership, but Thomas Richard Underwood, one of the number of young artists who were patronized by Dr. Munro, forms the connecting link.

Cotman made excursions into Surrey, and afterwards visited Wales. His first contributions to the Royal Academy, in 1800, were five drawings of views of Guildford and Dorking, and one of Harlech Castle ; in the two following years he sent further views in Wales. *Bridge, Valley, and Mountain* (Plate XXXIII), and *Llangollen* (Plate XXXIV), were probably produced from sketches made during his first visit to Wales. In the Horne Collection, exhibited at the Burlington Fine Arts Club, is a monochrome sketch of the latter subject, possibly made as a study for light and shade ; it lacks details which are of importance in the coloured drawing.

In 1802 Cotman visited Devonshire, and *Bridge at Saltram* (Plate XXXV), was painted about that time. Afterwards he returned to Norwich on a visit, and, following the example of Crome, sought to increase his income, by teaching. An advertisement in " The Norwich Mercury," September 1802, states: "Mr. Cotman informs his friends that during his stay in Norwich which will be for three weeks or a month, he proposes giving lessons in drawing to those ladies or gentlemen who may think his sketching from Nature or style of colouring beneficial to their improvement. Terms half a guinea an hour." In the three following years he made excursions to Yorkshire, Lincolnshire, and Durham, and *Durham Castle and Cathedral* (Plate XXXVI), *Greta Bridge* (Plate XXXVII), and *Windmill in Lincolnshire* (Plate XXXVIII), were the outcome of these visits.

Cotman produced several drawings of Durham Cathedral. In one, an upright picture at the British Museum, the noble pile in its romantic position is shown in bold relief, and not half hidden by the castle as in Mr. Colman's drawing. Both are severely produced in simple washes, whilst the grandeur of the architecture is finely depicted. There is also a drawing of *Greta Bridge* in the Reeve Collection ; though produced from the same sketch as the one shown here, there is evidence that neither was a replica of the other. A reproduction of this drawing accompanies the monograph on Cotman by Mr. Laurence Binyon in the Special Summer Number of THE STUDIO of 1903. A comparison of these two drawings, both executed in a quiet but severe manner, is most instructive. At this period Cotman appears to have had a partiality for bridges, for they frequently form a prominent feature in his paintings. The *Draining Mill, Lincolnshire*, an oblong drawing, also in the Reeve Collection, represents the same mill as that shown in Plate XXXVIII. In both drawings a light and warm tone prevails, and marks a transition to the hot sunshine pictures produced in later years.

In Yorkshire Cotman became acquainted with Mr. Francis Cholmeley of Brandsby, who took a warm interest in him and engaged him to teach the young Cholmeleys drawing. Cotman made some pencil portraits of them, showing he had already the idea of taking up portraiture, and he was turning his thoughts to oil painting. At this early date he had shown signs of those fits of despondency, which developed so seriously in later life, owing to the want of success in the sale of his water-colour paintings. In 1806 he made his last appearance at the Royal Academy, sending six of his north country drawings. The Old Water-Colour Society had been instituted in the previous year, and although Cotman did not join it, he probably felt a grievance, like other water-colour artists, at the scant manner with which their works were treated by the Royal Academy. At the end of this year Cotman determined to leave London and return to his native city. He took a house—now pulled down—in Luckett's Court, Wymer Street, and full of hope looked forward to a successful future by teaching and painting portraits.

The Norwich Society of Artists had been founded and its first exhibition held in the previous year. Cotman joined the Society and was doubtless a valuable addition to its members. To the Exhibition of 1807 he sent twenty drawings, some of them being portraits. He had now determined to become a portrait painter, and was so designated in the catalogue. In the next year he contributed no less than sixty-seven works. In addition to portraits were compositions, showing that Cotman was still striving after something fresh. One was a study for *The Waterfall* in the Reeve Collection, from which he subsequently produced the oil painting in Mr. Russell Colman's possession; it is a poetic composition, somewhat in the style of Wilson.

Cotman married Ann Miles, the daughter of a farmer at Felbrigg, in 1809, and as a means of further increasing his income he devised a scheme for circulating a collection of drawings, comprising six hundred works, on the plan of a circulating library. The quarterly subscription was one guinea, and Cotman announced he would "attend the delivery of the Drawings to Subscribers that he might facilitate their copying them by his instruction." Two years later Cotman removed to Southtown, Great Yarmouth, and whilst obtaining fresh pupils there he still continued to give drawing lessons at Norwich. At this period he appears to have devoted himself more to oil painting, and continued to do so spasmodically;

20

he never produced many works in this medium as he said "they consumed too much time." Several seascapes, however, were painted, notably *Fishing Boats off Yarmouth* in the Norwich Museum. The two other representative oil paintings by Cotman in that collection are *The Baggage Waggon* and *The Mishap*, both bequeathed by Mr. J. J. Colman. The charming painting *Boys Fishing* (Plate XLIX) was produced from a sketch entitled *Dewy Eve* in the Reeve Collection, British Museum.

Mr. Arthur Michael Samuel, M.P., a native of Norwich, and Lord Mayor of the city in 1912, possesses in his extensive collection of pictures an oil painting of the South Gate, Great Yarmouth, built in 1338. The towers having fallen out of the perpendicular and become unsafe, the fabric was sold in February 1812 to Mr. Jonathan Poppy for twenty-six pounds, to be pulled down. The picture bears Cotman's signature and date 1812, so it was presumably painted just prior to the demolition of the gateway. Cotman made an etching, dedicated to Dawson Turner, of this gate, and it appeared in "The Architectural Antiquities of Norfolk," Plate I, published in 1818. *Boats on Cromer Beach* (Plate XLVIII), another oil painting in Mr. Samuel's collection, shows a similarity in the handling of the brush, and certain like details are to be found in both pictures. There is a label on the back of the frame of the latter stating: "W. Boswell, late Thirtle, carver and gilder, Magdalen Street, Norwich," and Mr. Samuel is of opinion that Thirtle may have taken the picture over from Cotman, and being still unsold at the time of Thirtle's death, Boswell may have bought it from the widow, and then framed it for the person who ultimately purchased it. Also pasted at the back is the following advertisement: "Jan. 15th, 1825, Mr. J. S. Cotman recommences his course of teaching in the Departments of drawing, and painting in oil and water-colour, on 24th in Norwich, and in Yarmouth on 21st instant. St. Martin's at Palace." It is somewhat curious that the boats represented in the picture are not typical of those usually found at Cromer.

Cotman made three visits to Normandy in the years 1817, 1818, and 1820 to study Norman architecture, and during these tours, in addition to pencil drawings for his etchings, he made numerous sketches for water-colour paintings. Some of the latter he used on more than one occasion; for instance, a very similar drawing to *Dieppe* (Plate XXXIX) was on exhibition at Paterson's Galleries in 1913, and of *Mont St. Michel* (Plate XL) no less than four examples are recorded. Two of them were shown at the Norwich Art Circle Exhibition in 1888, and a third at the Burlington Fine Arts Club in the same year, the position of the group of figures and horses in the foreground varying slightly in each case. Since his visits to France his paintings were now executed in a brighter key.

Cotman disposed of his house at Yarmouth in 1823 and returned to Norwich, occupying a commodious residence at St. Martin's at Palace Plain. After having discontinued the sending of paintings to the Royal Academy, he had, up to this time, contributed works to the British Institution; but through the instigation of Miss Turner and her sister, Mrs. (afterwards Lady) Palgrave, Cotman was elected an Associate of the Society of Painters in Water-Colours in 1825, and his first contributions were *Dieppe* and *Mont St. Michel, showing the Phenomenon of the Mirage.*

At this period the fits of despondency, to which he was subjected, became more acute, owing to financial difficulties probably brought about by keeping up too large a house, and Dawson Turner in a letter to Cotman's father states : " The letter I had from him last night alarms me lest by brooding over his misfortunes his mind should actually become unhinged." Later, in refusing an invitation from a friend, Cotman wrote : " My views in life are so completely blasted, that I sink under the repeated and constant exertion of body and mind. Every effort has been tried, even without the hope of success ; hence that loss of spirits amounting almost to despair." Fortunately these fits of depression passed away and he was enabled to take a brighter view of life, and even at times became hilarious. In 1828 Cotman was engaged in the reopening of the Exhibition of the Norwich Society of Artists, which had been discontinued for two years owing to its old quarters being pulled down, and meanwhile a new gallery had been built. In announcing the opening it was stated that " Since its establishment the Norwich Society has shown 4,600 pictures, the work of 323 individuals, and while scarcely a single picture has been bought in the Norwich room—and the receipts at the door have never covered the expenses—the works of the very same artists have been readily purchased at the exhibitions in London, Edinburgh, Leeds, Liverpool, Manchester, Newcastle, and Carlisle." This complaint of the lack of patrons must surely have been disingenuous, when it is considered how both Crome and Cotman were assisted by the Gurneys and Harveys and other well-known Norfolk families. The name of the Society was changed to "The Norfolk and Suffolk Institution for the Promotion of Fine Arts"; Crome being dead, and James Stark and George Vincent having left the city, the spirit of the Norwich School had departed. Any painter with the slightest connexion with the Eastern Counties was invited to contribute works, and owing to easier communication with London, paintings by men who had none of the tradition of the School adorned the walls of the Exhibitions. Later Cotman and his fellow-artists inaugurated a series of conversaziones, of which he speaks as being a great success. In spite of this return of buoyant spirits all was not well. Towards the end of 1833 a vacancy occurred in the drawing-mastership at King's College School, London,

22

and principally through the influence of his friend Lady Palgrave, Cotman secured the appointment. Mr. Wedmore, in his "Studies of English Art," narrates how Turner was asked on three separate occasions by governors of the School whom they were to choose. His replies were, to the first, "Why, of course, Cotman"; to the second, "I have already said choose Cotman"; and to the last, "Whom are you to elect? I am tired of saying what I say again, Cotman! Cotman!! Cotman!!!" It is sad to think that a man with such brilliant talent should have been obliged to resort to the drudgery of teaching drawing during all his career in order to obtain a livelihood. Cotman, however, with renewed hopes, sold his possessions in Norwich, including a large collection of prints, books, and drawings, and settled in Hunter Street, Brunswick Square. Here, surrounded by friends, he enjoyed comparative ease for a time; but two years later he was compelled to sell at Christie's some drawings which he had collected, and in addition a few of his own works. The sale was a complete failure, few of the drawings fetching more than a pound apiece. He met, however, with some success in another direction. He obtained an appointment for his eldest son as assistant drawing-master at King's College School, which enabled Cotman to devote more time to painting, and he also was elected an Honorary Member of the Institute of British Architects.

At this period he turned his hand to painting figures and imaginary compositions, but they were not so successful as his landscapes. He paid periodical visits to his native city, and on the last occasion, in the autumn of 1841, he made some charming black-and-white studies. About twenty of them are in the Reeve Collection at the British Museum. One, *The Wold Afloat*, was executed with the great poetic feeling which he maintained to the last. Another study is *From my Father's House at Thorpe*, a view on the Yare looking towards Norwich. From it he commenced his last oil painting, *A View of the Norwich River*, dated January 18, 1842, now in the Castle Museum. It is quite unfinished, but it is valuable on account of its showing how, unlike Crome who always produced nature as he saw it, Cotman was always trying to improve on nature, the fir trees in the original sketch being replaced by poplars.

On his return from Norwich his health gradually gave way; he lingered on until July 21, 1842, when he died from sheer exhaustion. His remains were interred in the burial ground at the back of St. John's Wood Chapel. Another sale of his drawings was held at Christie's, and the result was as lamentable as the former one. Within half a century later, owing to the demand for drawings by Cotman, numerous spurious works were thrown on the market, and the Norwich Art Circle, on holding a loan exhibition of his pictures in 1888, found it necessary to announce that "the Council can confidently assert that every drawing attributed to him in this Exhibition is the genuine work of John Sell Cotman." The catalogue of this exhibition contains a valuable memoir of the artist by Mr. James Reeve.

Cotman was an ardent etcher. His earliest efforts on copper were probably soft ground etchings, which, with others produced later, were eventually published (1838) under the title of "Liber Studiorum," comprising forty-eight plates; thirty-nine were soft ground, of landscapes—*Millbank on the Thames* (Plate LII) being one of them—and the remainder hard ground, of figures. With respect to his hard ground etchings, as he himself said, he distinctly followed Piranesi. Between the years 1810 and 1820 he produced, in conjunction with his friend Dawson Turner, several series of etchings. The first set, issued in parts under the title of "Etchings by John Sell Cotman," was dedicated to Sir H. C. Englefield, Bart., and published by Boydell and Co., 1811. It comprises twenty-four plates, which, with one exception, are of architectural antiquities, principally in Yorkshire. The next set was "Norman and Gothic Architecture in Norfolk," a series of fifty plates completed and published in a volume in 1817. In the next year appeared "Architectural Antiquities of Norfolk," in which each plate, sixty in number, is dedicated to a patron. "Sepulchral Brasses of Norfolk" and "Antiquities of St. Mary's Chapel at Stourbridge, near Cambridge," were issued in 1819. The most important series, "Architectural Antiquities of Normandy," was issued after his visits to the district. It contains one hundred etchings, accompanied by historical and descriptive notices by Dawson Turner (see Plates L and LI). These etchings are interesting from an architectural point of view, as the subjects were selected for that purpose, whilst a few of them are treated pictorially. At Yarmouth Cotman illustrated with etchings a small volume giving an account of the Grand Festival at Yarmouth on Tuesday, April 19, 1814, held to celebrate the fall of Napoleon. He also produced a large plate of Nelson's Monument at Yarmouth, when the foundation stone was laid in 1817. Cotman's copperplates were bought at the sale at Norwich in 1834 by H. G. Bohn, who subsequently issued them as a collective edition.

PLATE XXXIII

"BRIDGE, VALLEY, AND MOUNTAIN." WATER-COLOUR BY JOHN SELL COTMAN (16¼ × 11 INCHES)

(In the British Museum, London)

PLATE XXXIV

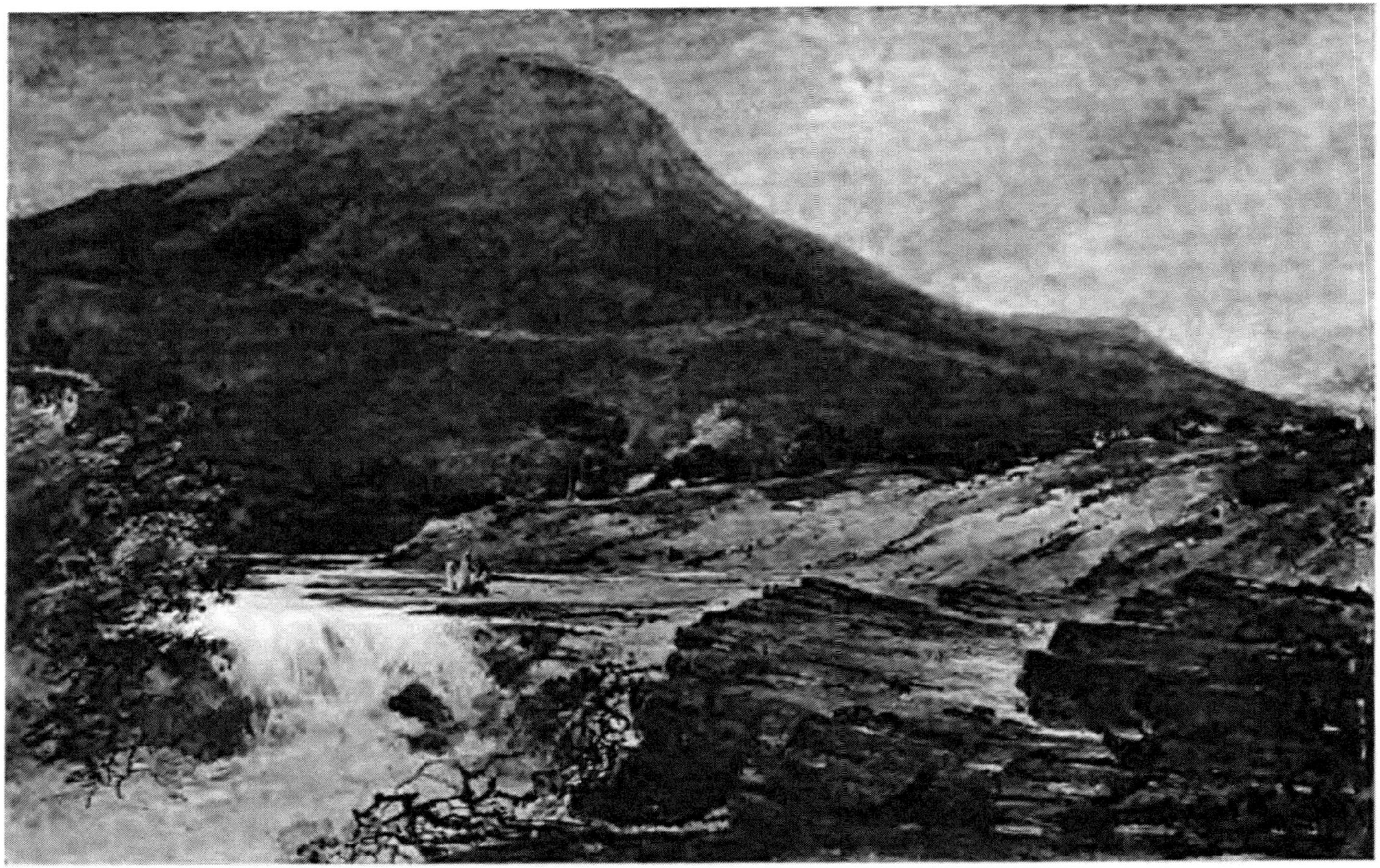

(*In the possession of A. P. Oppé, Esq.*)

"LLANGOLLEN." WATER-COLOUR BY JOHN SELL COTMAN ($11\frac{1}{8} \times 7\frac{1}{8}$ INCHES)

PLATE XXXV

"BRIDGE AT SALTRAM, DEVONSHIRE." WATER-COLOUR BY JOHN BELL COTMAN (10⅜ × 7⅛ INCHES)

(In the British Museum, London)

PLATE XXXVI

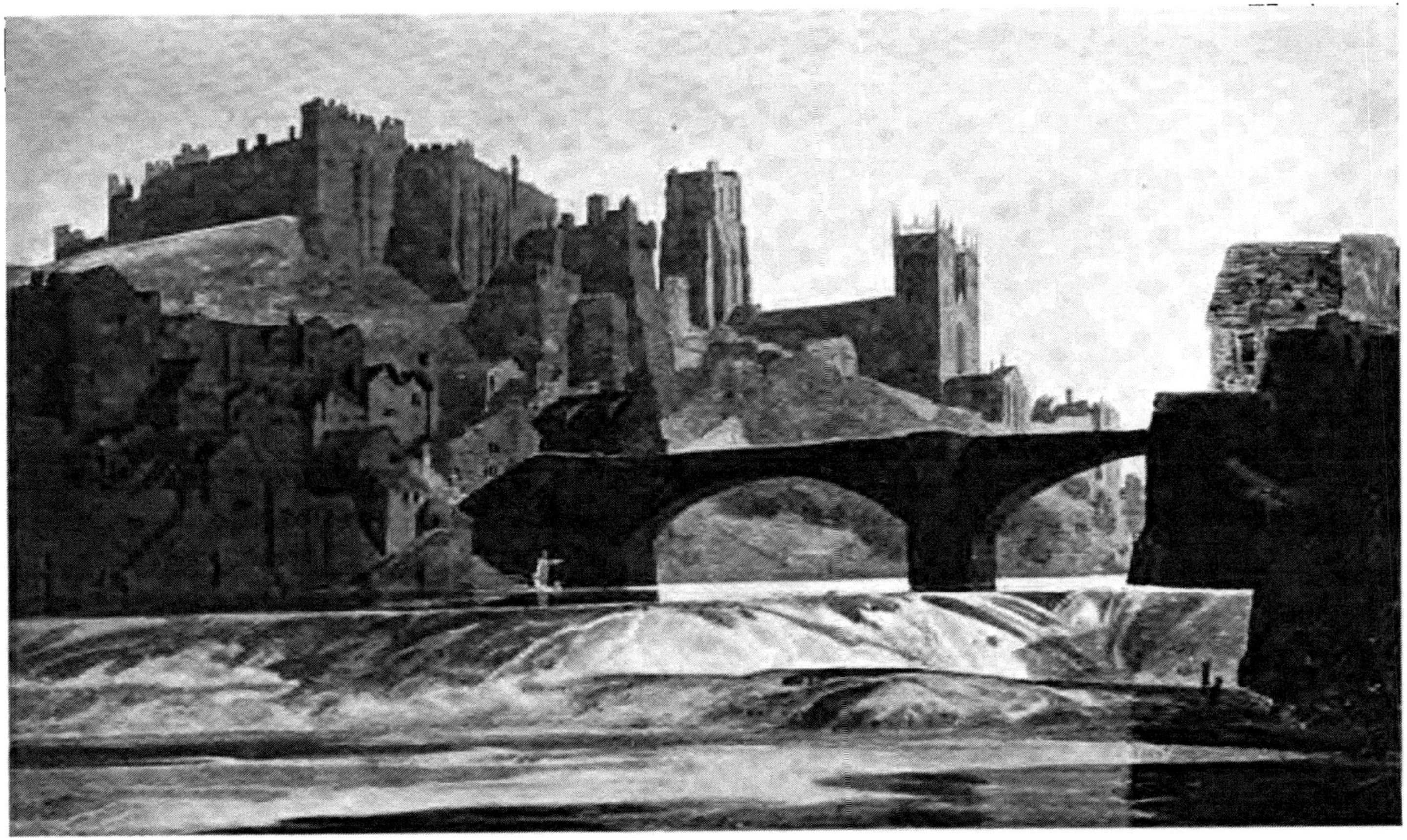

(In the possession of Russell J. Colman, Esq.)

"DURHAM CASTLE AND CATHEDRAL." WATER-COLOUR BY JOHN SELL COTMAN ($20\frac{3}{4} \times 12\frac{1}{2}$ INCHES)

PLATE XXXVII

"GRETA BRIDGE, YORKSHIRE." WATER-COLOUR BY JOHN SELL COTMAN (19¾ × 11¾ INCHES)

(In the possession of Russell J. Colman, Esq.)

PLATE XXXVIII

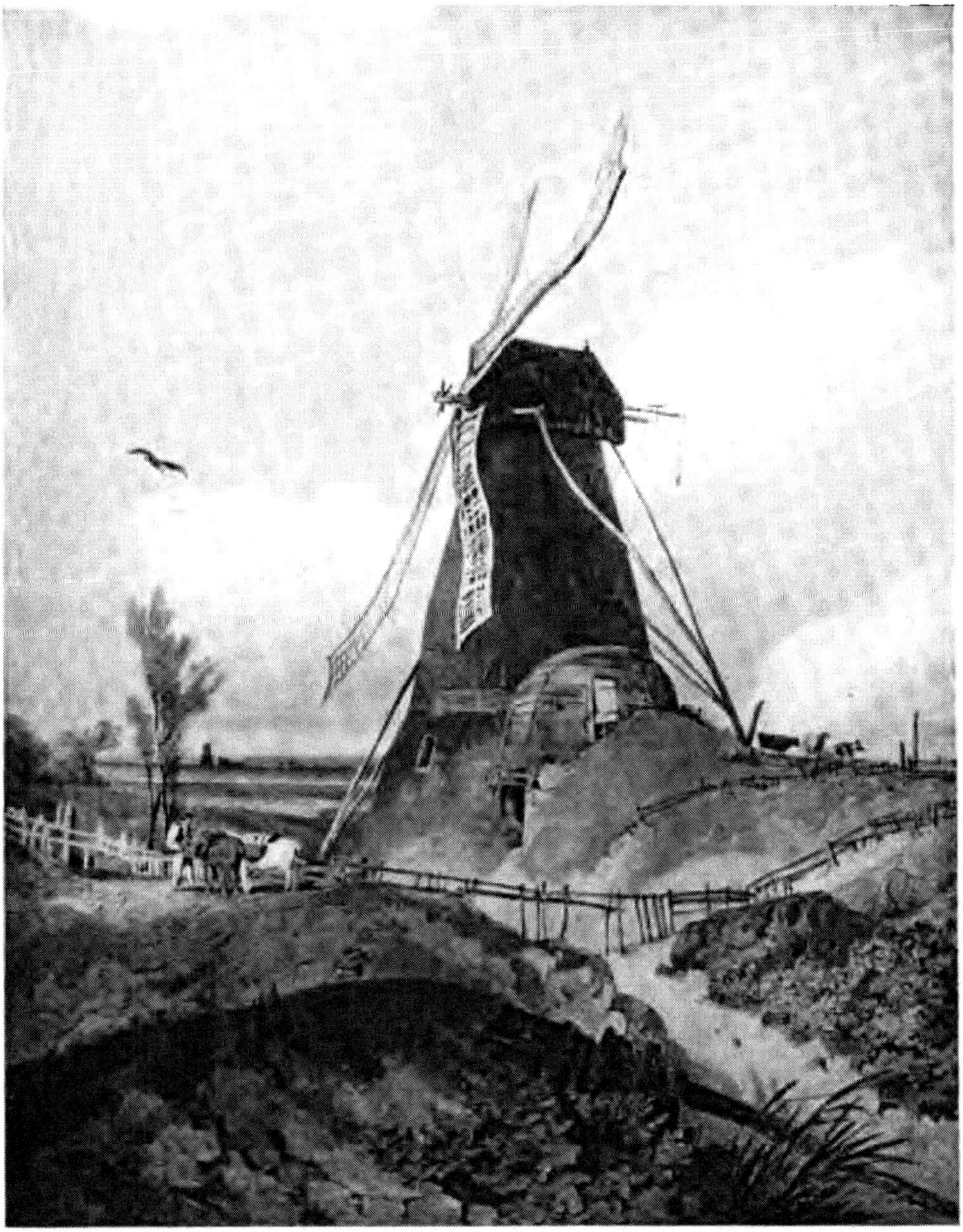

(In the Victoria and Albert Museum, London)

"WINDMILL IN LINCOLNSHIRE." WATER-COLOUR BY JOHN SELL COTMAN (15¼ × 19 INCHES)

PLATE XXXIX

"DIEPPE." WATER-COLOUR BY JOHN SELL COTMAN (21 × 11¾ INCHES)

(In the Victoria and Albert Museum, London)

PLATE XL

"MONT ST. MICHEL." WATER-COLOUR BY JOHN SELL COTMAN (21 × 12 INCHES)

(*In the possession of R. W. Lloyd, Esq.*)

PLATE XLI

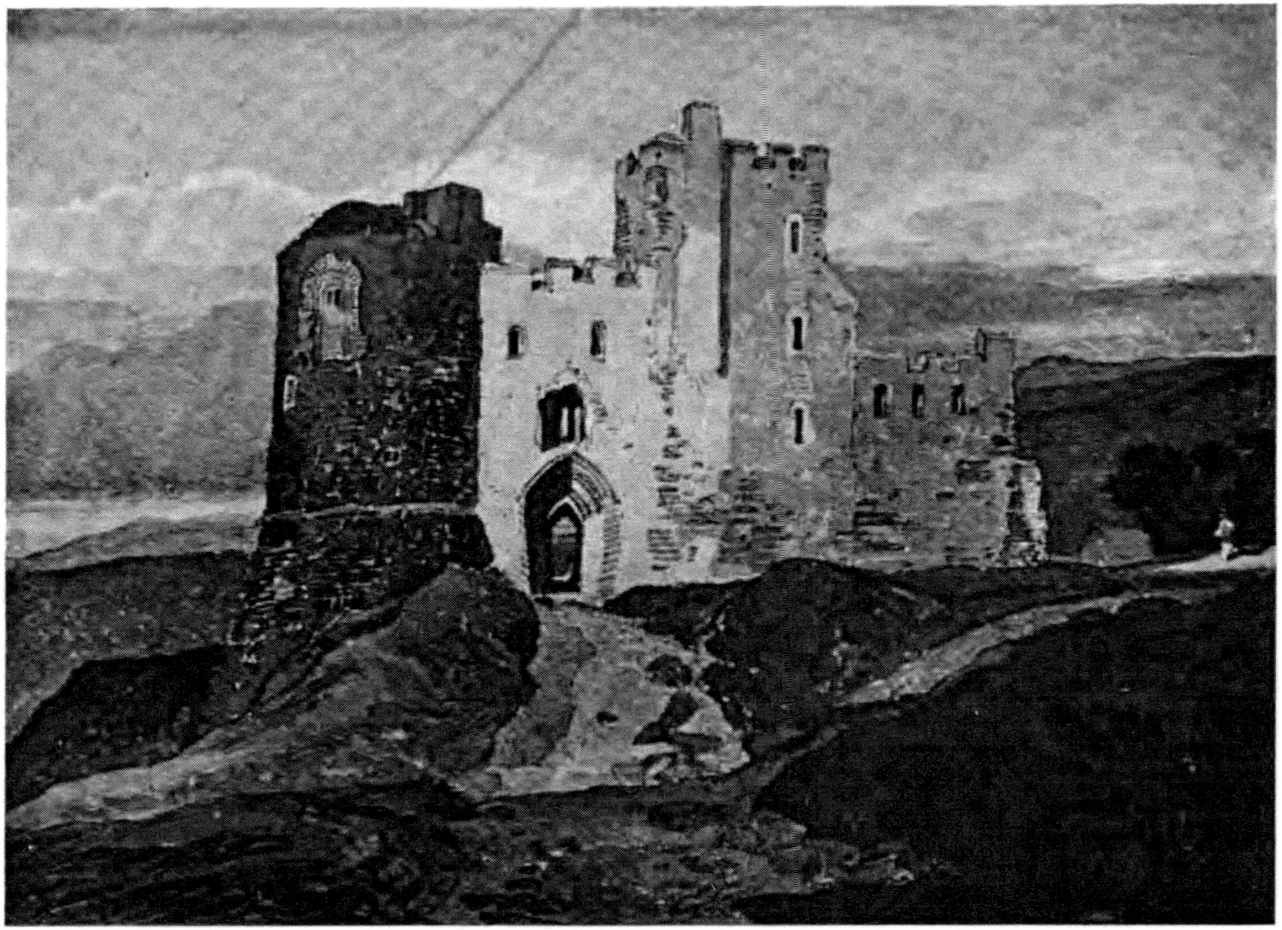

(In the British Museum, London)

"POWIS CASTLE." WATER-COLOUR BY JOHN SELL COTMAN ($10\frac{1}{8} \times 7\frac{1}{4}$ INCHES)

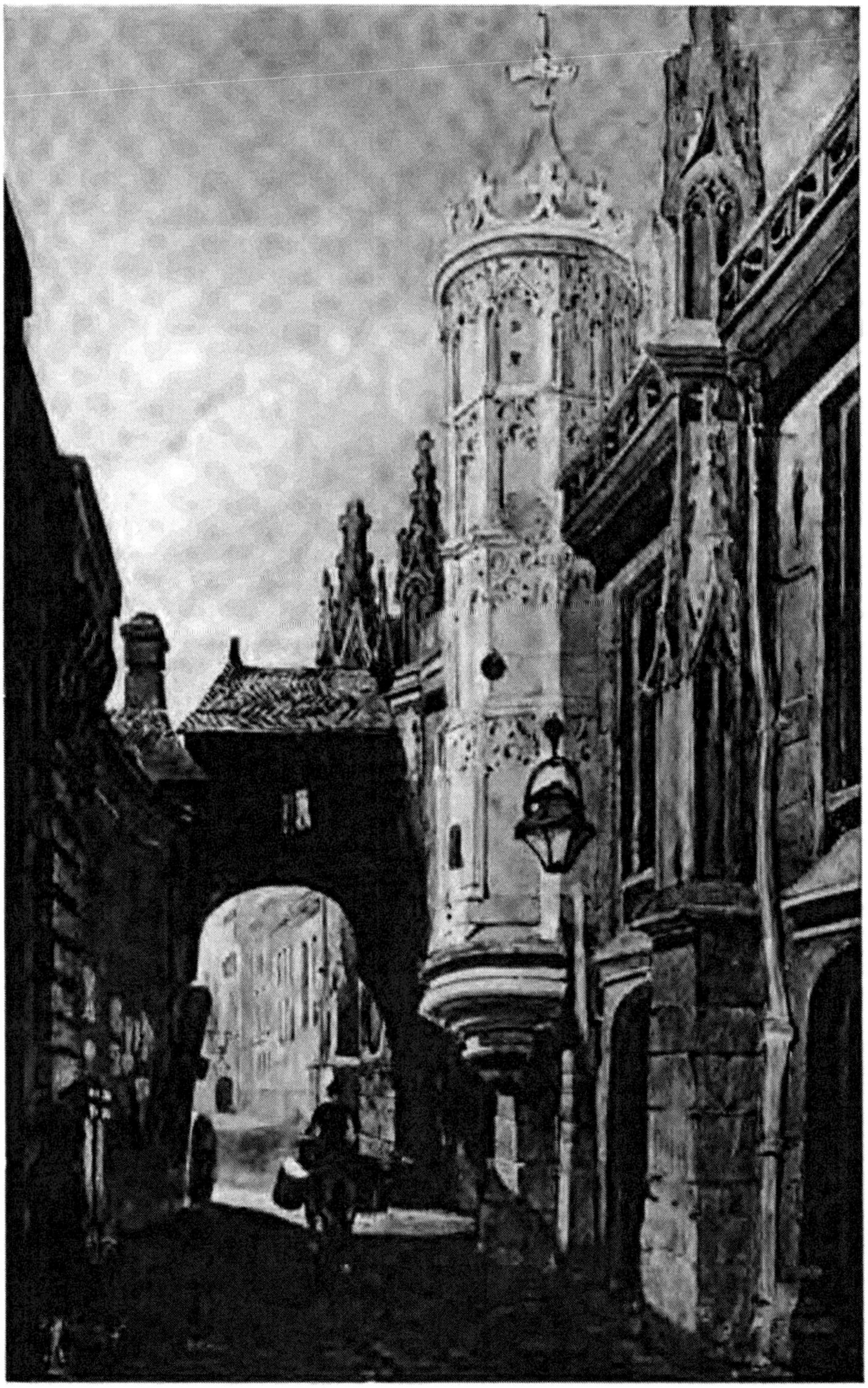

(In the Victoria and Albert Museum, London)

"THE PALAIS DE JUSTICE AND THE RUE ST. LÔ, ROUEN"
WATER-COLOUR BY JOHN SELL COTMAN (9¾ × 14¼ INCHES)

PLATE XLIII

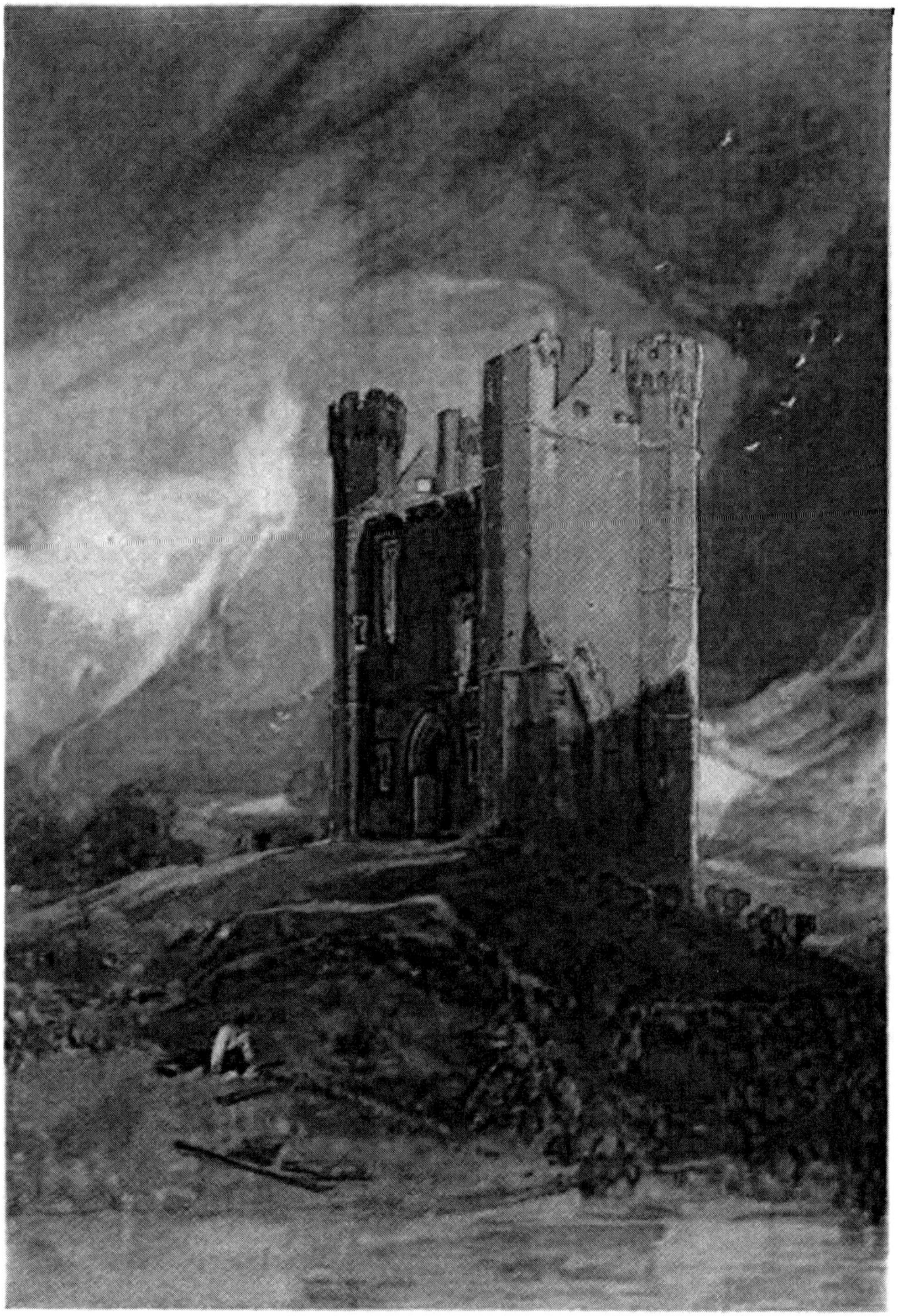

(In the possession of F. W. Smith, Esq.)

"RUINED CASTLE NEAR A STREAM." WATER-COLOUR BY JOHN SELL COTMAN (12¼ × 18¾ INCHES)

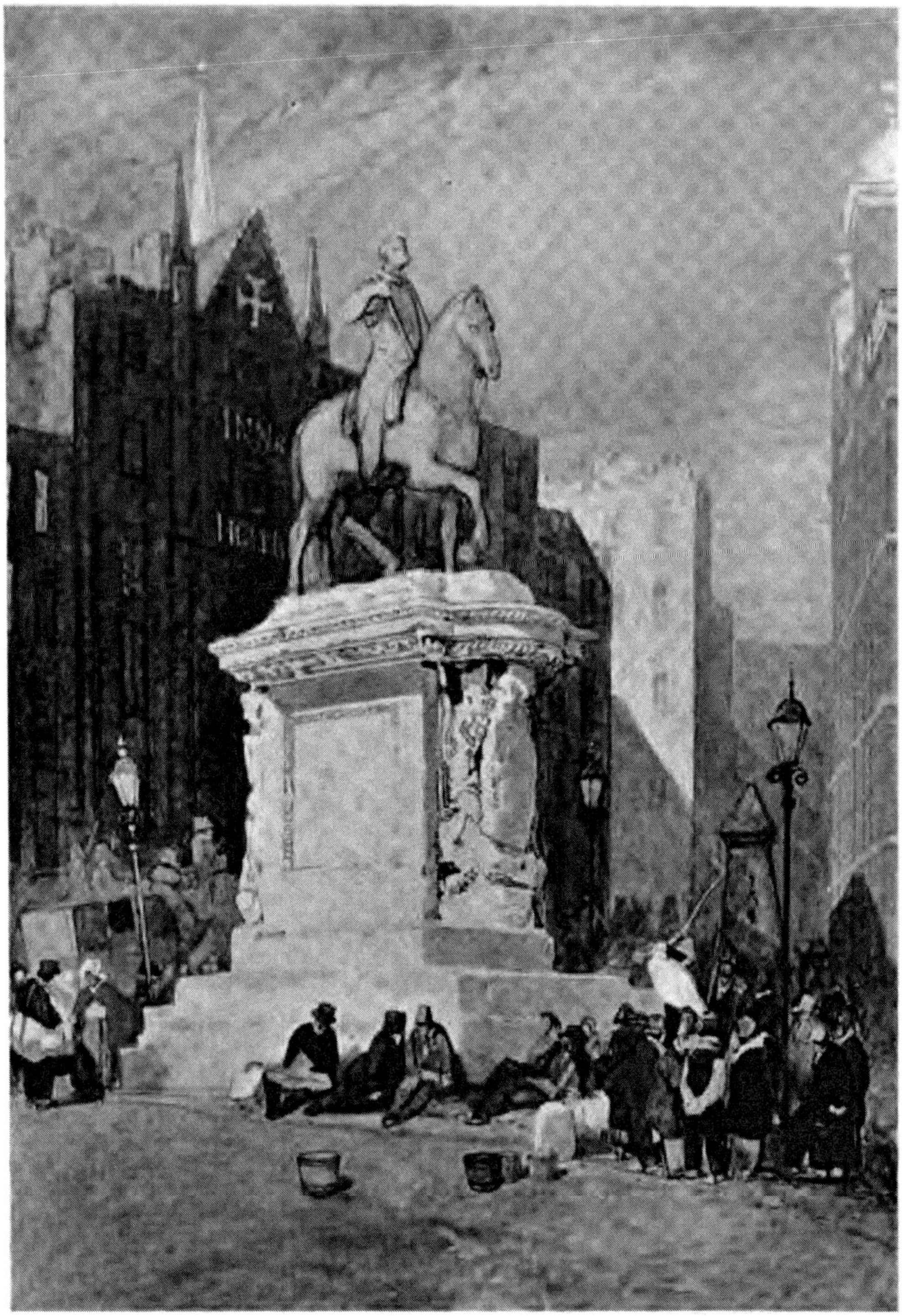

(In the possession of Russell J. Colman, Esq.)

"STATUE OF CHARLES I, CHARING CROSS." WATER-COLOUR BY JOHN SELL COTMAN (12¼ × 18¼ INCHES)

PLATE XLV

"CADER IDRIS." WATER-COLOUR BY
JOHN SELL COTMAN (17½ × 13½ INCHES)

PLATE XLVI

"ETON COLLEGE." WATER-COLOUR BY JOHN SELL COTMAN (12¾ × 8¾ INCHES)

(In the British Museum, London)

PLATE XLVII

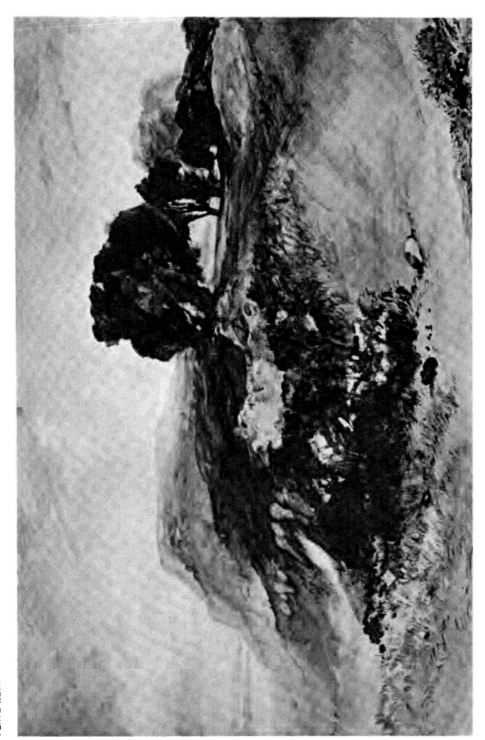

WATER-COLOUR STUDY BY JOHN SELL COTMAN (13¾ × 8¼ INCHES)

(*In the possession of Russell J. Colman, Esq*)

PLATE XLVIII

"BOATS ON CROMER BEACH." OIL PAINTING BY JOHN SELL COTMAN (35½ × 25 INCHES)

In the possession of
Arthur Michael Samuel, Esq., M.P.)

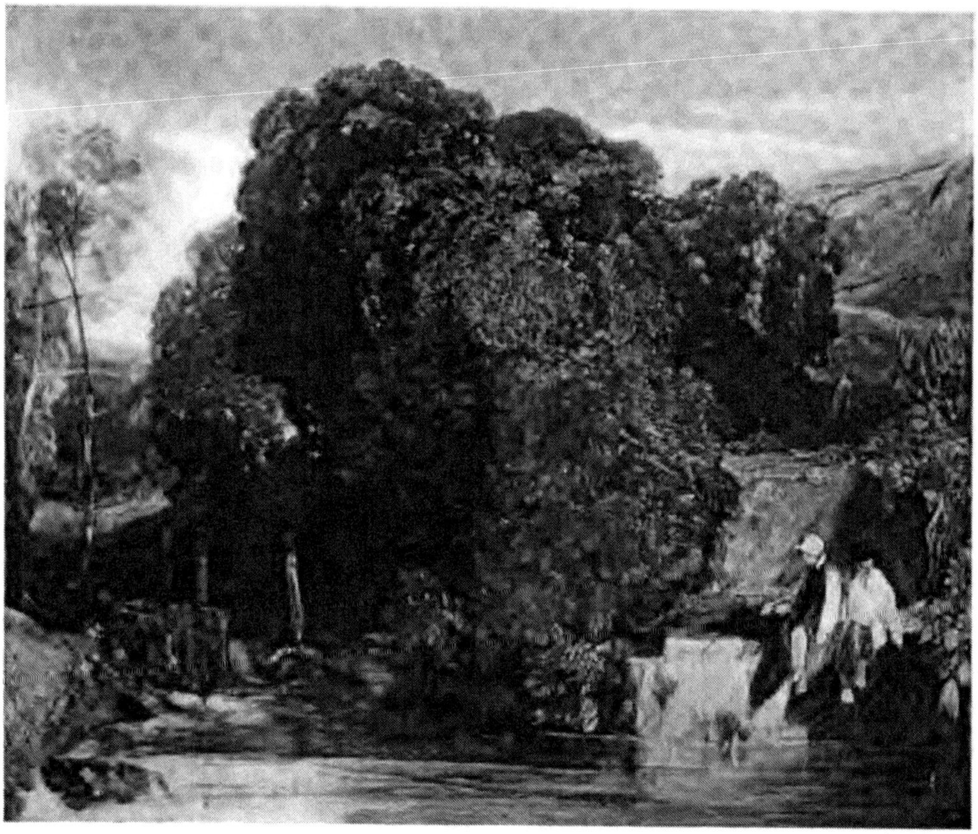

(In the possession of Russell J. Colman, Esq.)

"BOYS FISHING." OIL PAINTING BY JOHN SELL COTMAN (17×13½ INCHES)

PLATE L

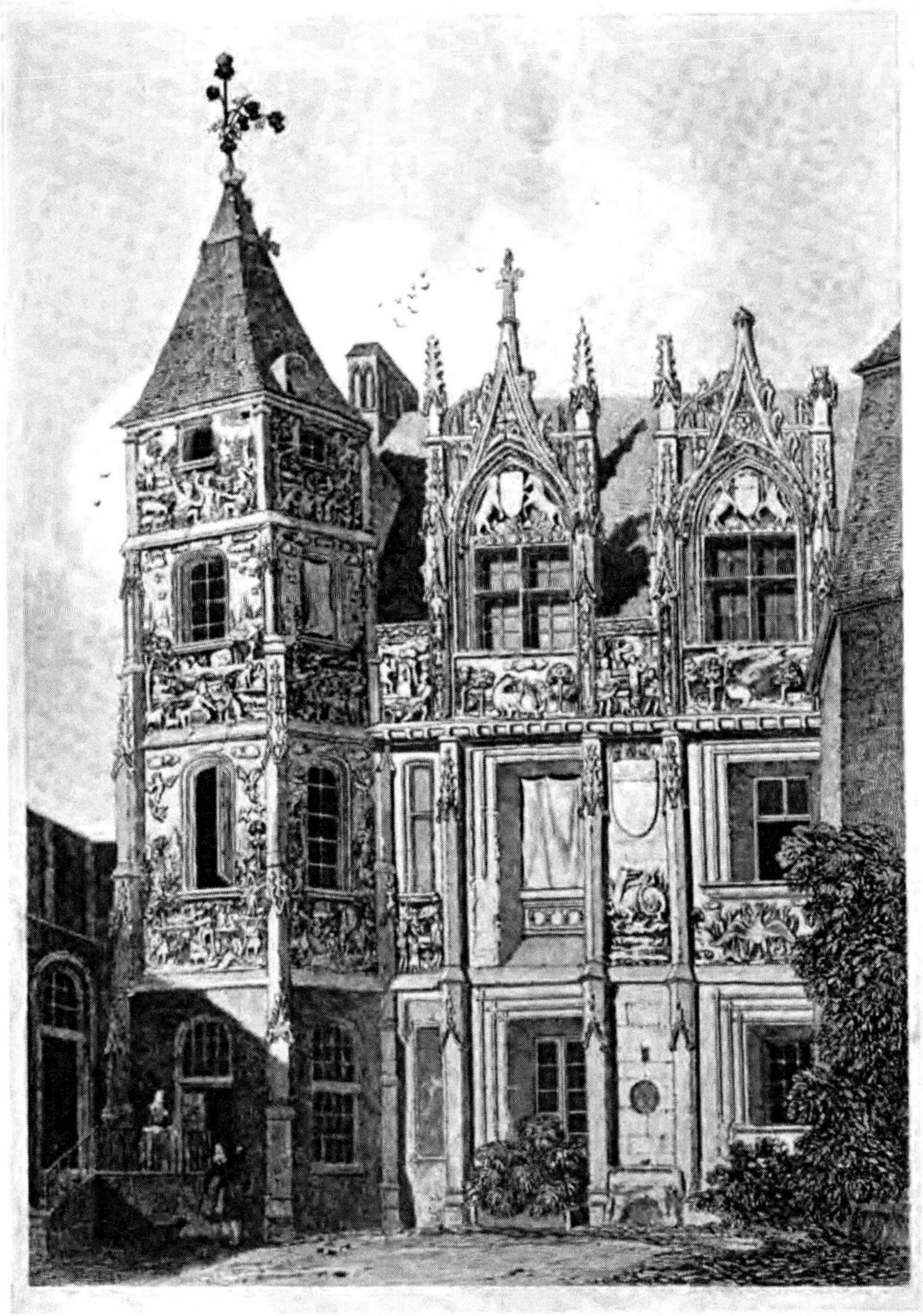

(From an impression in the Victoria and Albert Museum, London)

"HOUSE IN THE PLACE DE LA PUCELLE AT ROUEN." ETCHING BY JOHN SELL COTMAN

PLATE LI

"CHÂTEAU AT FONTAINE-LE-HENRI, NEAR CAEN." ETCHING BY JOHN SELL COTMAN

(From an impression in the Victoria and Albert Museum, London)

PLATE LII

"MILLBANK ON THE THAMES." ETCHING BY JOHN SELL COTMAN

(From an impression in the Victoria and Albert Museum, London)

OTHER MEMBERS OF THE NORWICH SCHOOL

JAMES STARK

James Stark was articled by his father to "Old" Crome, and a friendship which sprang up between the master and pupil existed until the end of the former's life. After the apprenticeship Crome continued to give practical advice to Stark, and his letters to him are of considerable interest in showing his views on the treatment of composition. In 1816 he wrote:

" . . . . In your letter you wish me to give you my opinion of your picture. I should have liked it better if you had made it more of a whole—that is, the trees stronger, the sky running from them in shadow up to the opposite corner; that might have produced what, I think, it wanted, and have made it much less a too picture effect. I think I hear you say, this fellow is very vain, and that nothing is right that does not suit his eye. But be assured what I have said I thought on the first sight, it strengthened me in that opinion every time I looked at it. (Honesty, my boy !) So much for what it wanted ; but how pleased I was to see so much improvement in the figures, so unlike our Norwich School, I may say they were good. Your boat was too small for them (you see I am at it again), but then the water pleased me, and I think it would not want much alteration in the sky. I cannot let your sky go off without some observation. I think the character of the clouds too affected—that is, too much of some of our modern painters, who mistake some of our great masters because they sometimes put in some of those round characters of clouds, they must do the same ; but if you look at any of their skies, they either assist in the composition or make some figure in the picture, nay sometimes play the first fiddle. I have seen this in Wouverman's and many others I could mention.
Breath (breadth ?) must be attended to, if you paint but a muscle give it breath. Your doing the same by the sky, making parts broad and of good shape, that they may come in with your composition, forming one grand plan of light and shade, this must always please a good eye and keep the attention of the spectator and give delight to everyone. Trifles in nature must be overlooked that we may have our feelings raised by seeing the whole picture at a glance, not knowing how or why we are so charmed. I have written this long rigmarole story about giving dignity to whatever you paint—I fear so long that I should be scarcely able to understand what I mean myself ; you will, I hope, take the word for the deed, and at the same time forgive all faults in diction, grammar, spelling, &c. &c. &c. . . . Believe me, dear James, Yours, &c. &c., John Crome."

On another occasion he wrote :

"Do not distress us with accidental trifles in nature, but keep the masses large and in good and beautiful lines, and give the sky, which plays so important a part in all landscape, and so supreme a one in our low level lines of distance, the prominence it deserves, and in the coming years the posterity you paint for shall admire your work"

James Stark was born in Norwich in 1794, and was the youngest son of Michael Stark, a native of Scotland, who had settled in that city and carried on the business of a dyer. He was educated at the Grammar School, where he met as a school-fellow John Berney Crome, and through the son the boy first became aquainted with "Old" Crome. Never enjoying robust health, he was allowed to follow his own devices and took up painting at an early age. In 1811 he was sufficiently advanced, although only sixteen, to have his first contribution accepted by the Royal Academy. In the following year he was elected a member of the Norwich Society and became a regular contributor to the exhibitions.

Afterwards Stark came to London and entered the Academy Schools. He contributed paintings to the British Institution, where in 1818 he gained a premium of fifty pounds. About two years later he returned to Norwich and devoted himself to painting the scenery around the city—*Whitlingham, from Old Thorpe Grove* (Plate LIII), *Thorpe Wood* (Plate LIV), and *The Forest Gate* (Plate LVII) are examples of his work at this period. Stark executed a series of paintings for a work on "Scenery of the Rivers of Norfolk," comprising the Yare, the Waveney and the Bure. They were engraved by George and William John Cooke and others, and published in 1834, four years after his return to London.

Stark founded his art on a study of the Dutch landscape painters, and on the instruction which he received from his master. He chose simple rural scenes, but in the treatment of his subjects he had not the breadth and richness of Crome. In 1840 he removed to Windsor, and whilst residing there his style underwent a change, and to a great extent the feeling of the Norwich School disappeared. He eventually returned to London, for the purpose of his son's education in art, and died there on 24th March, 1859. His remains were taken to Norwich and buried in the Rosary Cemetery. To a certain extent James Stark's reputation suffers from his best works being attributed to Crome, whilst inferior paintings are ascribed to him. The Norwich Art Circle held a loan exhibition of his works in 1887.

Stark's son, Arthur James, who was born at Chelsea in 1831, became a painter of landscapes and of animals. He used to occasionally insert cattle in his father's pictures.

GEORGE VINCENT

The early career of George Vincent was very similar to that of Stark. The son of a Norwich shawl manufacturer, he was born in 1796. He was educated at the Grammar School and afterwards received instruction in art from Crome. In the years 1811 and 1812 he contributed to the exhibition at Sir Benjamin Wrench's Court works described as "after Crome," and under his master's guidance he made rapid progress in painting in oils. He exhibited fifteen works at Norwich in 1814, besides sending a painting to the Royal Academy.

Two years later Vincent left Norwich and took up his residence in London. He exhibited landscapes at the British Institution and at the Society of Painters in Water-Colours, which at this period was throwing open its doors to oil paintings. At the same time he continued his connection with

26

Norwich by sending pictures to the annual exhibitions. In 1822 he married and went to reside at Kentish Town. He did not, however, remain there long, as, according to correspondence preserved in the Reeve Collection, he was residing at Upper Thornhaugh Street, Bedford Square, in 1824, and was contemplating painting sketches of the battles of the Nile and Trafalgar, for which prizes had been offered by the Directors of the British Institution. "The Norfolk hero gained those battles, and shall it be said that Norfolk artists would not contend for the prize now offered?" wrote Vincent. But owing to intemperance and financial difficulties his intentions were never carried out, and at the end of the year he found himself a prisoner in The Fleet. Friends came to his rescue, and through one of them Vincent obtained a commission to paint a large picture of *Greenwich Hospital*. He produced a noble painting, but until it was shown at the International Exhibition in 1862, thirty years after the artist's death, his talents as a landscape painter had received but slight recognition.

Little further is known concerning Vincent's life and in 1831 he disappeared. In the catalogue of the Society of British Artists in the following year "deceased" is added after his name, so it may be presumed that he had died. Nothing is definitely recorded of the time or place of his death. Vincent visited Scotland on one occasion and produced a few landscapes of Scottish scenery, but the majority of his exhibited works are views of Norfolk, and *Trowse Meadows* (Plate LIX) and *Whitlingham, looking towards Norwich* (Plate LVIII) are good examples showing his style of painting. He also produced some etchings. Vincent was a finer artist than Stark, his paintings are broader and have more atmospheric effect in them, and if he had not given way to intemperate habits he would probably have ranked amongst the foremost of British landscape painters.

JOHN BERNEY AND WILLIAM HENRY CROME

John Berney, the eldest son of "Old" Crome, was born at Norwich in December 1794. His father, realizing his own deficiency, determined his son should have a sound education, and sent him to the Grammar School, where he remained until eighteen years of age. At the same time, with a view to becoming a painter, he accompanied his father on his sketching tours. In 1816 he went with his school-fellow, George Vincent, and Mr. Steel, a doctor, who afterwards married Miss Crome, on an excursion to Paris. Later John assisted his father in teaching, and was appointed landscape painter to the Duke of Sussex. He became a member of the Norwich Society and was appointed Vice-President in 1818 and subsequently President on several occasions.

On the death of "Old" Crome the son continued in the profession of teaching and occupied his father's house in Gildengate Street, to which

27

he added a studio. In conjunction with John Sell Cotman, he took a lively interest in the re-opening of the Norwich Society in 1828. Owing, however, to his extravagant habits John Berney Crome became a bankrupt in 1831, when the contents of his father's house were sold, and many of "Old" Crome's paintings and his own works were disposed of at the time. He retired to Great Yarmouth where he continued to teach drawing until his death, which took place in September 1842.

John Berney Crome was a man of genial character and of jovial disposition. His portrait, painted by H. B. Love, hangs in the Castle Museum, Norwich. His work shows the influence of his father, and he painted many moonlight effects, the *River Scene by Moonlight* (Plate LXIII), executed in 1834, being a characteristic example.

William Henry Crome, the third son of "Old" Crome, was born in 1806. He also was a pupil of his father, and for a time assisted his brother in teaching. He exhibited at the British Institution and the Society of British Artists, but does not appear to have obtained any great success.

ROBERT LADBROOKE AND HIS SONS, HENRY AND JOHN BERNEY LADBROOKE

Born at Norwich in 1770, Robert Ladbrooke was apprenticed to a printer and engraver. In early life he became associated with John Crome, the two being of about the same age, and for many years they were great friends. When still boys they entered into a partnership and hired a garret for a studio. Later Ladbrooke married Mary Berney, the sister of Crome's wife, and this event helped to cement the friendship.

Robert Ladbrooke assisted Crome in the formation of the Norwich Society of Artists, and contributed annually to the earlier exhibitions. In 1816, however, a bitter quarrel arose which terminated their friendship, and the Norwich Society of Artists was for a time divided into two camps. It appears that Robert Ladbrooke proposed that the profits of the exhibitions should be devoted to purchasing casts and any other works or art in order to lay the foundation of an Academy, at which members might study and improve themselves. Crome, on the other hand, was desirous of continuing to spend the money on monthly meetings in the evenings, at which supper should be provided, for the discussion of art topics. The result was that Ladbrooke seceded from the Society and took with him James Sillett, J. Clover, John Thirtle, Joseph Stannard and others. They engaged a hall at the Shakespeare Tavern on Theatre Plain and held a separate exhibition. It was called "The Twelfth Exhibition of the Norfolk and Norwich Society of Artists," whilst the twelfth exhibition of the original Society was continued, as before, at Sir Benjamin's Wrench's Court. Norwich could not support two art institutions, and after its third

28

venture the rival Society was compelled to close its doors. Most of the seceders returned to the original Society, but Robert Ladbrooke never exhibited there again during the lifetime of Crome.

Most of Ladbrooke's early paintings were executed on small panels, somewhat in the style of "Old" Crome (see *Beach Scene, Mundesley*, Plate LXI), but cannot be compared with those of the friend of his younger days. During the greater part of his career he was a successful drawing-master, but eventually gave up the profession in favour of two of his sons. He resided all his life in Norwich and died there in 1842. For some years he had been engaged in making drawings of the Churches of Norfolk which were lithographed and published in five volumes by Charles Muskett, of Norwich, in the year after his death.

Henry and John Berney Ladbrooke, the second and third sons of Robert Ladbrooke, followed their father's career. The former was born in 1800 and the latter in 1803. They were both pupils of their uncle, Crome, as well as of their father. Henry became a drawing-master, first at North Walsham and afterwards at Lynn. He painted landscapes in oil, somewhat in the style of his father, but they were not numerous. He died in 1869. John Berney taught drawing at Norwich, where he built himself a house on Mousehold Heath, and where he died in 1879. In his landscapes (see Plates LXIV and LXV) he was influenced by his uncle, but the painting is hard and wanting in atmosphere. Both the brothers contributed works to the exhibitions of the Norwich Society of Artists.

JOHN THIRTLE

Like Crome, John Thirtle was the son of poor parents. He was one of those who assisted the master in the formation of the Norwich Society of Artists, but afterwards appears to have become more intimate with Cotman. In 1812 he married Elizabeth Miles, sister of Cotman's wife. He was the son of a Norwich bootmaker and was born there in 1777. In early life he was sent to London, where, it is believed, he learned the trade of frame-making. On his return to his native city he opened a shop for the sale of prints in Magdalen Street. After a while he added to his business that of a carver and gilder. He also became a drawing-master and a miniature painter. His contributions to the early exhibitions of the Norwich Society were principally miniatures, but afterwards he became a landscape painter in water-colours. He is chiefly noted for his river scenes, mostly of the Yare and the Wensum, of which *Whitlingham Reach* (Plate LXX), in which the first steamboat plying from Norwich to Yarmouth is depicted, and a *View Under Bishop's Bridge, Norwich* (Plate LXXII) are good examples. He was fond of introducing storm effects into his pictures (see *Cromer, looking East*, Plate LXXI), and when a thunderstorm passed over

29

Norwich he would watch it from Castle Hill. During the latter part of his life Thirtle suffered from an affection of the lungs, and after a long illness, which greatly interfered with his sketching, he died in 1839. The Norwich Art Circle, in 1886, held a loan exhibition of his paintings.

ROBERT DIXON

A native of Norwich, Robert Dixon was born in 1780. He went to London early to study at the Royal Academy, and on his return to Norwich he was for a time engaged in scene-painting at the theatre. Afterwards he became a drawing-master. He painted landscapes in water-colour, as well as architectural subjects and compositions; he was one of the contributors to the first exhibition of the Norwich Society, of which he was Vice-President in 1809. He produced a series of etchings on soft ground in 1810–11 of views of "Norfolk Scenery." He died in 1815 at the early age of thirty-five, and a few weeks after his death an exhibition of his works was held at Sir Benjamin Wrench's Court.

CHARLES AND DAVID HODGSON

These artists, father and son, were both staunch supporters of Crome and the Norwich Society of Artists, although their art lay in an entirely different direction to that of the master. The father, Charles Hodgson, born in the latter half of the eighteenth century, became mathematical master at the Norwich Grammar School and taught drawing. His works were of an architectural character, and he was appointed architectural draughtsman to the Duke of Sussex.

David Hodgson, born in 1798, became the drawing-master at the Grammar School, and to a certain degree followed in his father's footsteps; but his paintings assumed a more domestic character, in which buildings were the chief feature (see *Old Fish Market, Norwich*, Plate LXVI). He held the appointment of painter of domestic architecture to the Duke of Sussex. He died in 1864 at Norwich where he had lived all his life.

HENRY NINHAM

John Ninham was an heraldic painter and copper-plate printer. His son Henry, born at Norwich in 1793, was brought up in his father's profession, and was for many years employed in painting armorial bearings on coaches. Later he painted to a small extent both in oil and water-colours, chiefly views of Norwich (see *Fishgate Street, Norwich*, Plate LXVII) and architectural subjects, many of which he contributed to the Norwich Society's exhibitions. He is also known for his etchings, which he executed in a careful and precise manner. He assisted other etchers in Norwich in biting and proving their plates. Several works containing etchings and lithographs by him were published. He died in 1874 and was buried at Norwich.

30

JOSEPH AND ALFRED STANNARD

The two brothers Joseph and Alfred Stannard were both painters. The elder, Joseph, born in 1797, received his art education from Robert Ladbrooke, and became chiefly a marine painter (see *Fishing Boats*, Plate LXVIII). A large picture, *Thorpe Water Frolic, Afternoon*, in the Castle Museum, Norwich, was his most important work. He executed some etchings which were published in a volume, entitled "Norfolk Etchings," in 1827. He was always delicate and died in 1830.

Alfred Stannard was nine years younger than his brother Joseph, with whom he studied, but the works of the two brothers are not similar. During his career he was chiefly occupied in teaching, but he painted pastoral scenes as well as some views on the coast (see *Yarmouth Jetty*, Plate LXIX). He contributed to the exhibitions of the Norwich Society, besides sending a few works to the British Institution and Society of Artists. He died at Norwich at the advanced age of eighty-three. His son, Alfred George, painted in the style of his father, and his daughter, Eloise Harriet, executed still-life subjects.

MILES EDMUND AND JOHN JOSEPH COTMAN

As in the case of Crome's eldest son, Cotman's firstborn was given his mother's maiden name at his christening. Miles Edmund, born at Norwich in 1810, became a pupil and companion of his father, John Sell Cotman. He commenced when a boy of thirteen to send drawings to the exhibitions of the Norwich Society, and continued to do so until the Society ceased to exist. He painted both in oil and water-colours, and his works, in which he followed the style of his father's earlier paintings, are distinguished for their preciseness (see *Boats on the Medway*, Plate LXXV, and *Trowse Mills*, Plate LXXVI). When J. S. Cotman left Norwich to become the drawing-master at King's College School, he handed over his teaching connection in Norwich to his eldest son. Later, Miles Edmund came to London to assist at King's College School, and eventually succeeded his father as drawing-master there. Owing to ill health he was obliged to relinquish the post and he returned to his native city to reside with his brother, John Joseph, at Thorpe until 1835 when the two brothers removed to Great Plumstead, on the outskirts of Norwich. After teaching at North Walsham for some years, he died in 1858.

John Joseph Cotman was born in 1814 at Southtown, Great Yarmouth. He was placed with his uncle, a haberdasher in London Street, but possessing the same early proclivities as his father, he spent much of his time in wandering about the country making sketches. He accompanied his father to London in 1834, but returned again to Norwich to take over the teaching connection from his brother Miles, when the latter went to

31

King's College School. From a journal which J. J. Cotman kept (now in the Reeve Collection), it may be gathered that he was subject to ungovernable fits of temper and wanting in stability, and as he says "one of the defects in my character is now, and has been, indecision and want of perseverance." This was certainly the case, as an entry "My plan is now to rise at seven and get two hours work before breakfast," is followed by "Rose late, nothing done before breakfast—not even shaved." He executed a few oil paintings, but is better known for his water-colours (see *Whitlingham, looking towards Norwich*, Plate LXXVII). Unlike his brother's work, they are executed in a free manner, and in many of them blue is extensively used. Suffering from cancer, he was obliged to enter the Norfolk and Norwich Hospital, and died there in 1878.

THOMAS LOUND

Born in 1802, Thomas Lound was engaged in a brewery at Norwich. He was also a successful amateur painter of landscapes, both in oil and water-colours, receiving his instruction in art from John Sell Cotman. He became a member of the Norwich Society in 1818 and contributed annually until its close. Later he exhibited at the Royal Academy and British Institution. His paintings were executed in a free manner—see *Ely Cathedral* (Plate LXXVIII) and *St. Benet's Abbey* (Plate LXXIX). He died in 1861 at Norwich.

Brief reference must be made to other artists who were connected with Norwich, but whose work in no manner represents the famous School of Painting. EDWARD THOMAS DANIELL belonged to a Norfolk family. He was sent to the Norwich Grammar School, where he was taught drawing by Crome. He also received lessons from J. S. Cotman. Although Daniell was ordained a priest, he became a painter and excelled in etching. He went on an exploring expedition to the East and died in 1842 from fever in Asia Minor. HENRY BRIGHT, born at Saxmundham, went to Norwich where he was apprenticed to Paul Squire, a chemist. He took up art and eventually removed to London. JAMES SILLETT, a painter of still-life subjects; JOSEPH CLOVER, a portrait painter; DANIEL COPPIN, chiefly a copyist; MICHAEL W. SHARP, a portrait and *genre* painter; ROBERT LEMAN, an amateur; ANTHONY SANDS and his son, FREDERICK A. SANDS (afterwards SANDYS), the portrait painter; ALFRED PRIEST, a pupil of James Stark, whose style he copied (see *Godstow Bridge, Oxford*, Plate LXXX); JOHN MIDDLETON, a pupil of Henry Bright; and JAMES WILLIAM WALKER, an art-master.

PLATE LIII

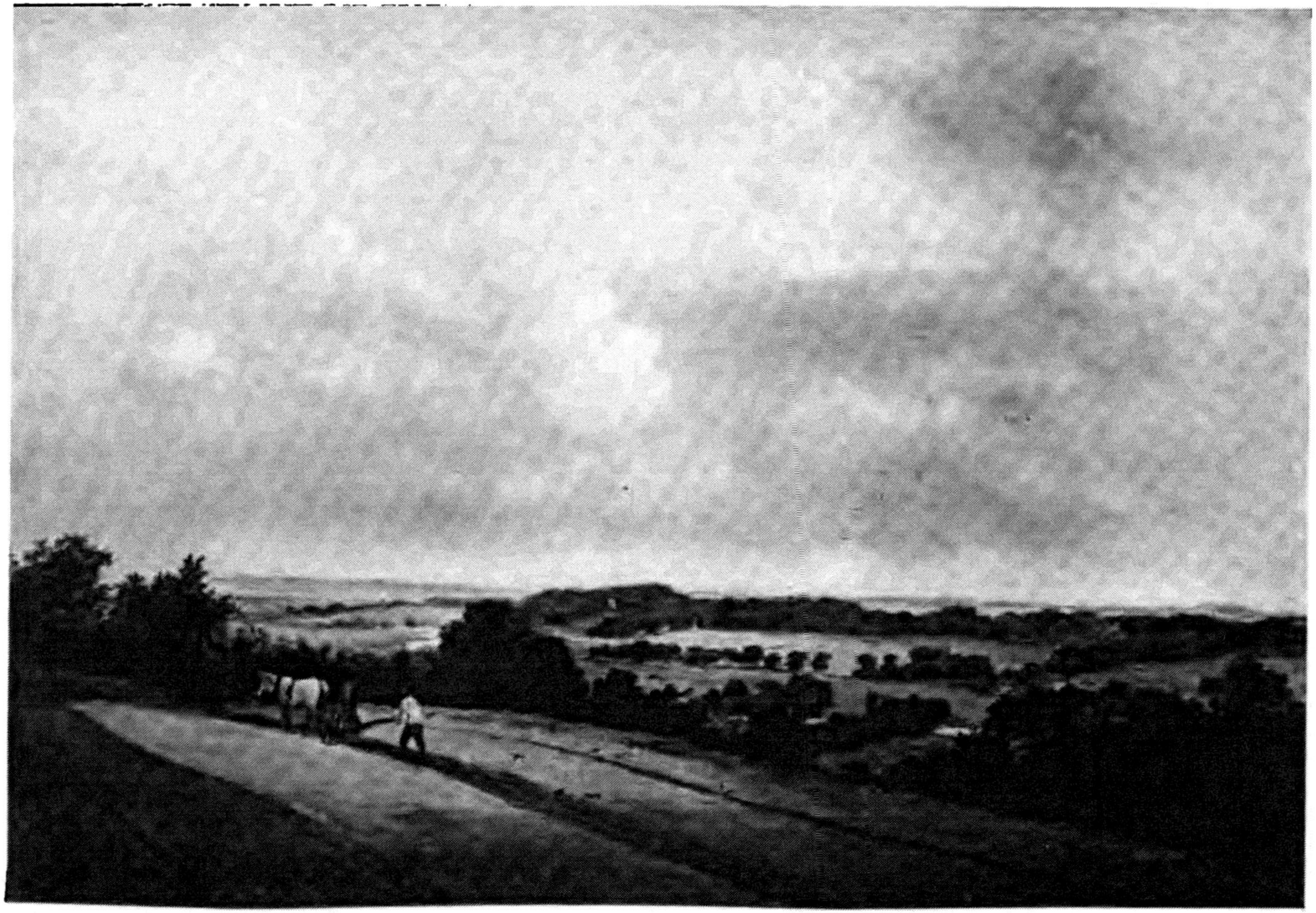

(In the possession of Russell J. Colman, Esq.)

"WHITLINGHAM, FROM OLD THORPE GROVE." OIL PAINTING BY JAMES STARK ($23\frac{1}{2} \times 16\frac{3}{8}$ INCHES)

PLATE LIV

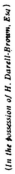

"THORPE WOOD." OIL PAINTING BY JAMES STARK (15 × 12 INCHES)

(In the possession of H. Darell-Brown, Esq)

PLATE LV

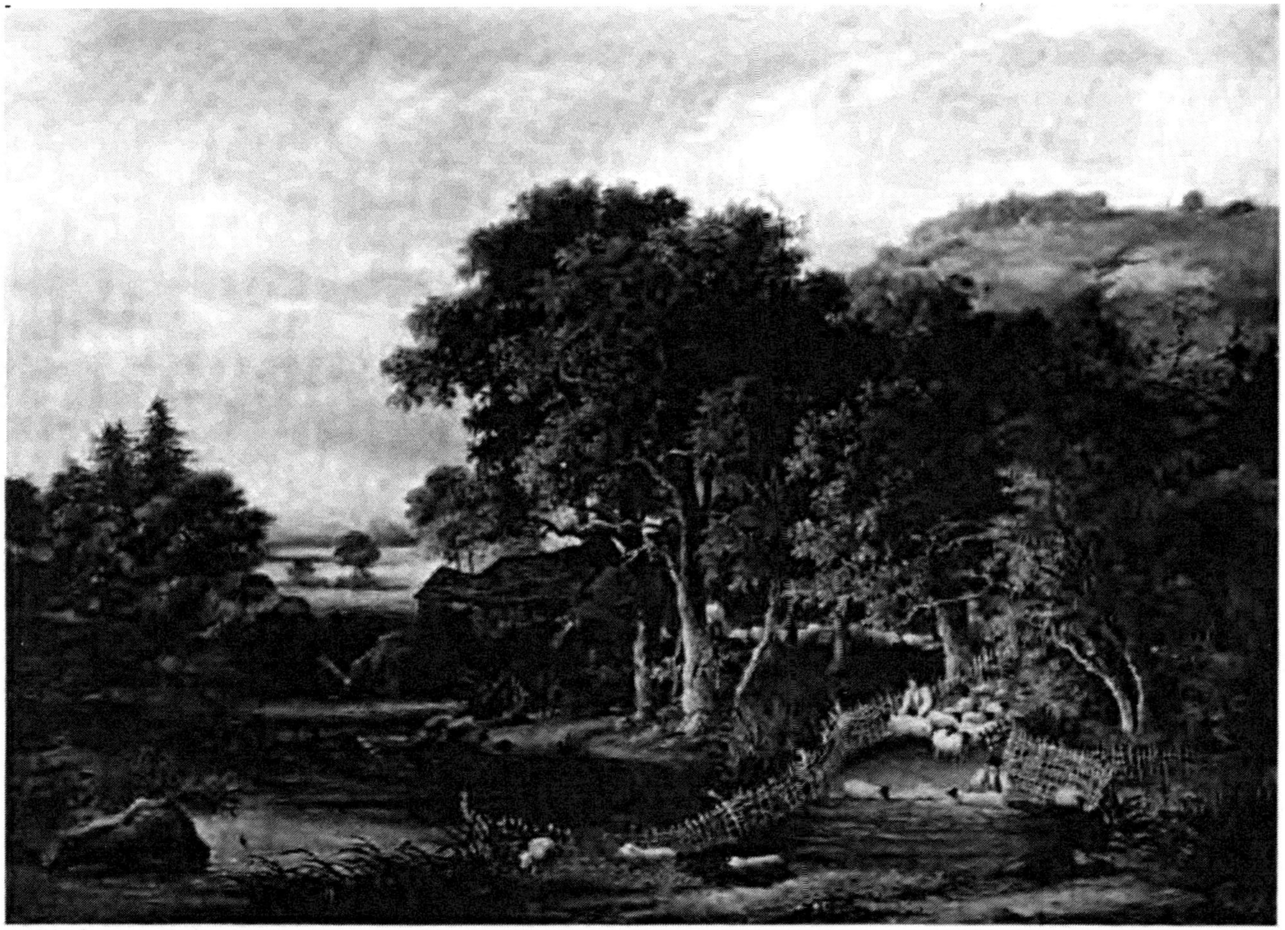

(In the possession of Russell J. Colman, Esq.)

"SHEEP WASHING." OIL PAINTING BY JAMES STARK ($31\frac{3}{4} \times 23\frac{1}{2}$ INCHES)

PLATE LVI

"LANDSCAPE WITH CATTLE." OIL PAINTING BY JAMES STARK (22 × 16 INCHES)

(In the possession of John H. McFadden, Esq.)

PLATE LVII

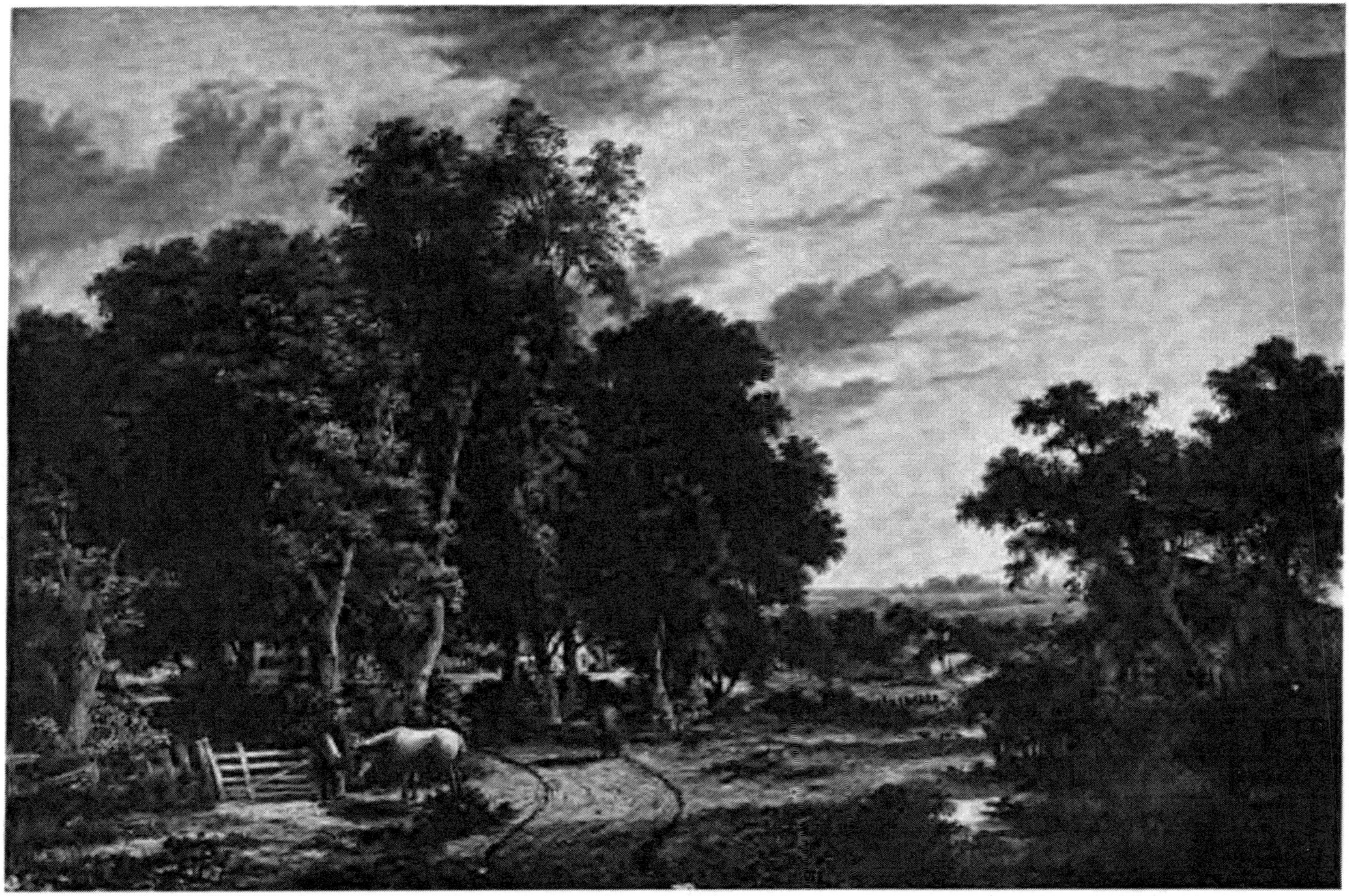

(In the Castle Museum, Norwich. Colman Bequest)

"THE FOREST GATE." OIL PAINTING BY JAMES STARK (29½ × 20 INCHES)

PLATE LVIII

"WHITLINGHAM, LOOKING TOWARDS NORWICH." OIL
PAINTING BY GEORGE VINCENT (39½ × 29½ INCHES)

(In the Possession of Russell J. Colman, Esq.)

PLATE LIX

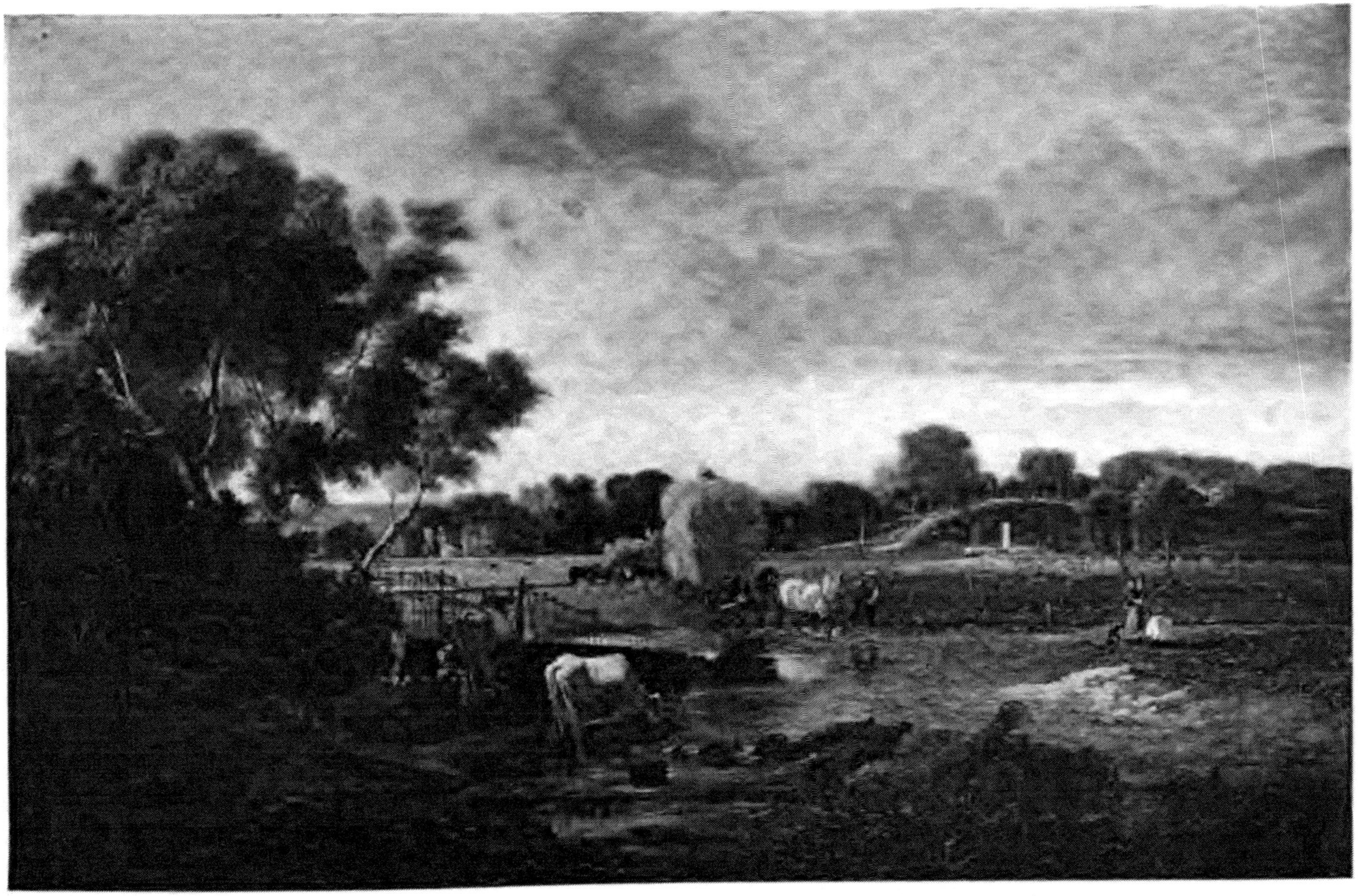

(*In the Castle Museum, Norwich. Colman Bequest*)

"TROWSE MEADOWS, NEAR NORWICH." OIL PAINTING BY GEORGE VINCENT (36½ × 28½ INCHES)

PLATE LX]

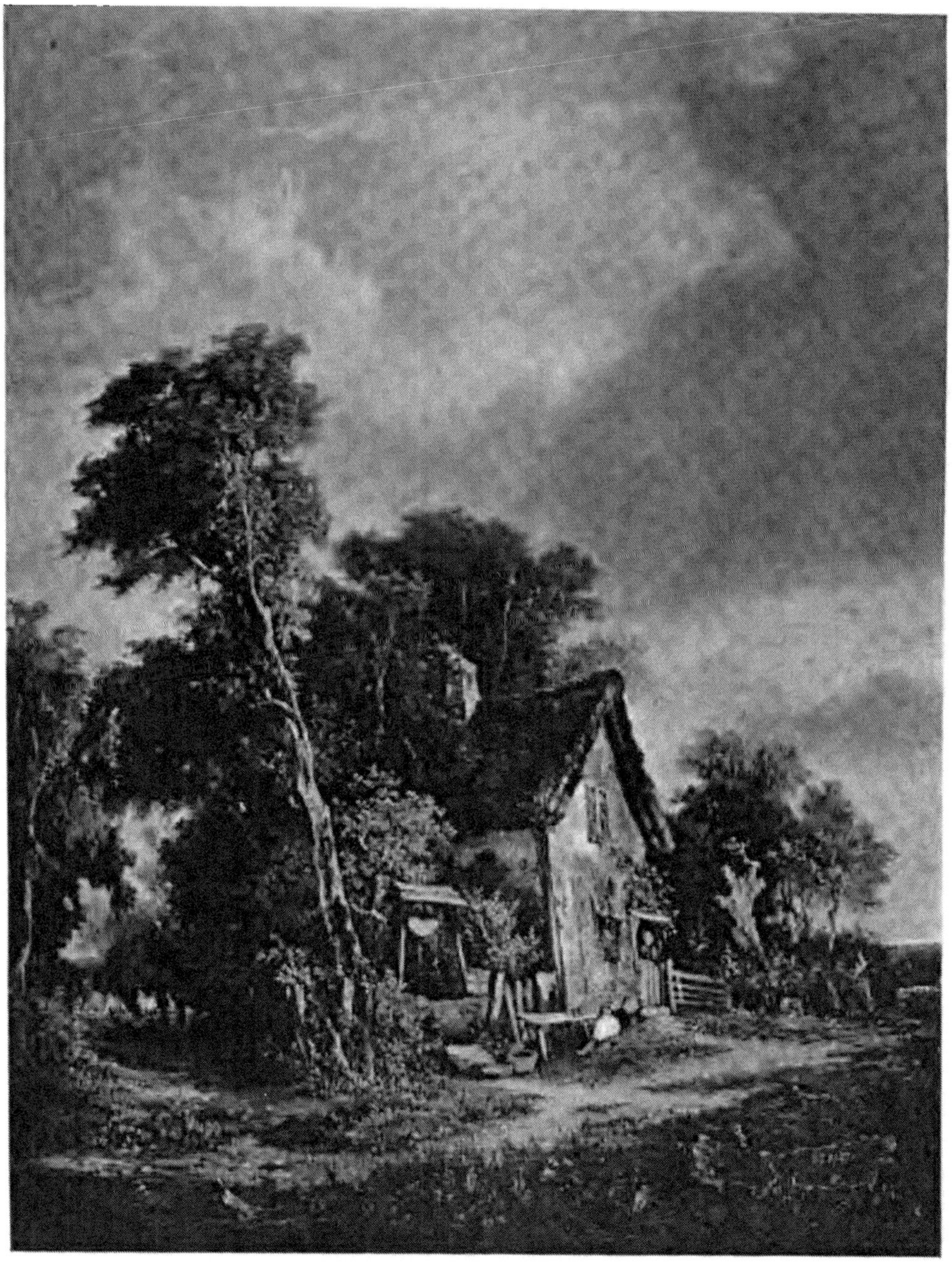

(*In the possession of*
H. Darell-Brown, Esq.)

"COTTAGE AND WELL." OIL PAINTING
BY GEORGE VINCENT (15½ · 20 INCHES)

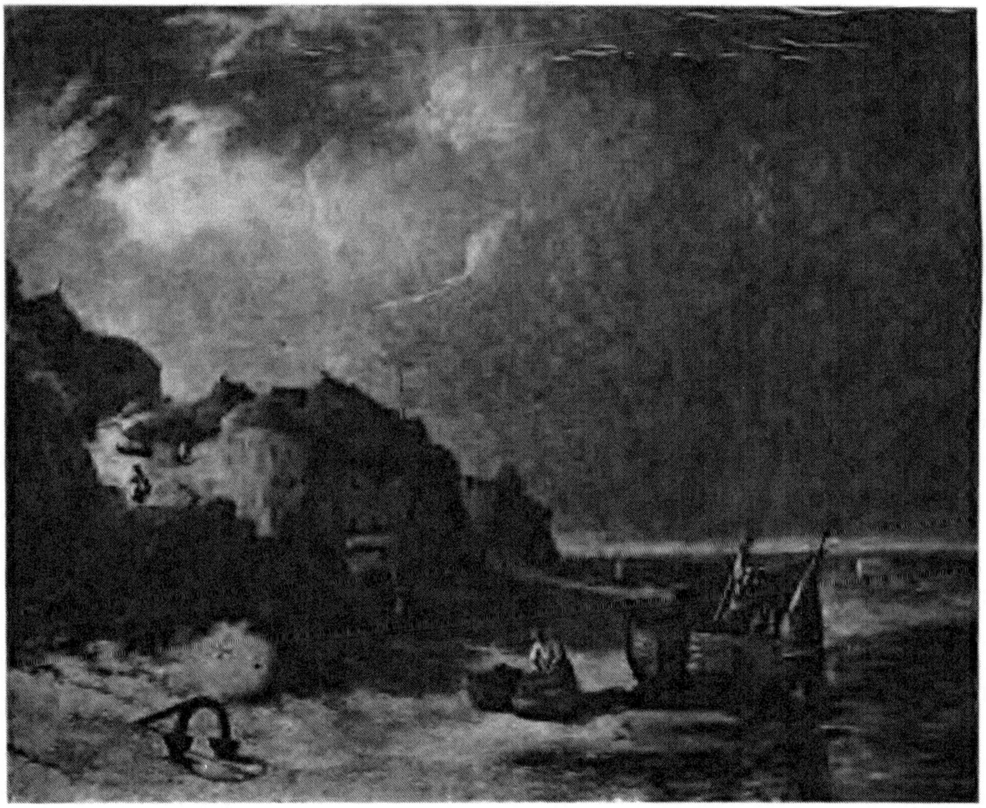

(In the possession of Russell J. Colman, Esq.)

"BEACH SCENE, MUNDESLEY." OIL PAINTING BY ROBERT LADBROOKE (24 × 19½ INCHES)

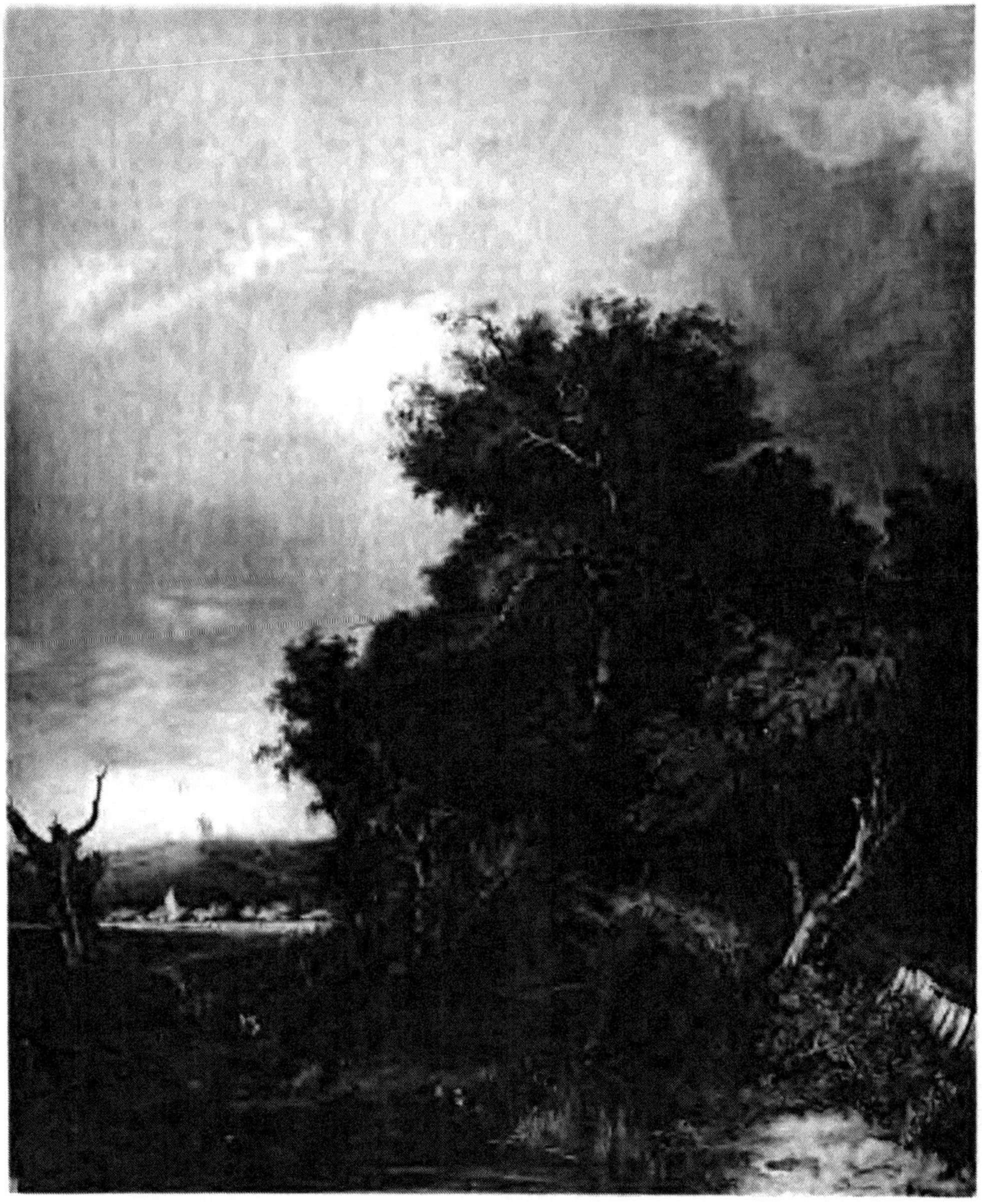

(*In the Castle Museum, Norwich*)

"VIEW NEAR BURY ST. EDMUNDS"
OIL PAINTING BY JOHN BERNEY
CROME (30½ × 37⅝ INCHES)

PLATE LXIII

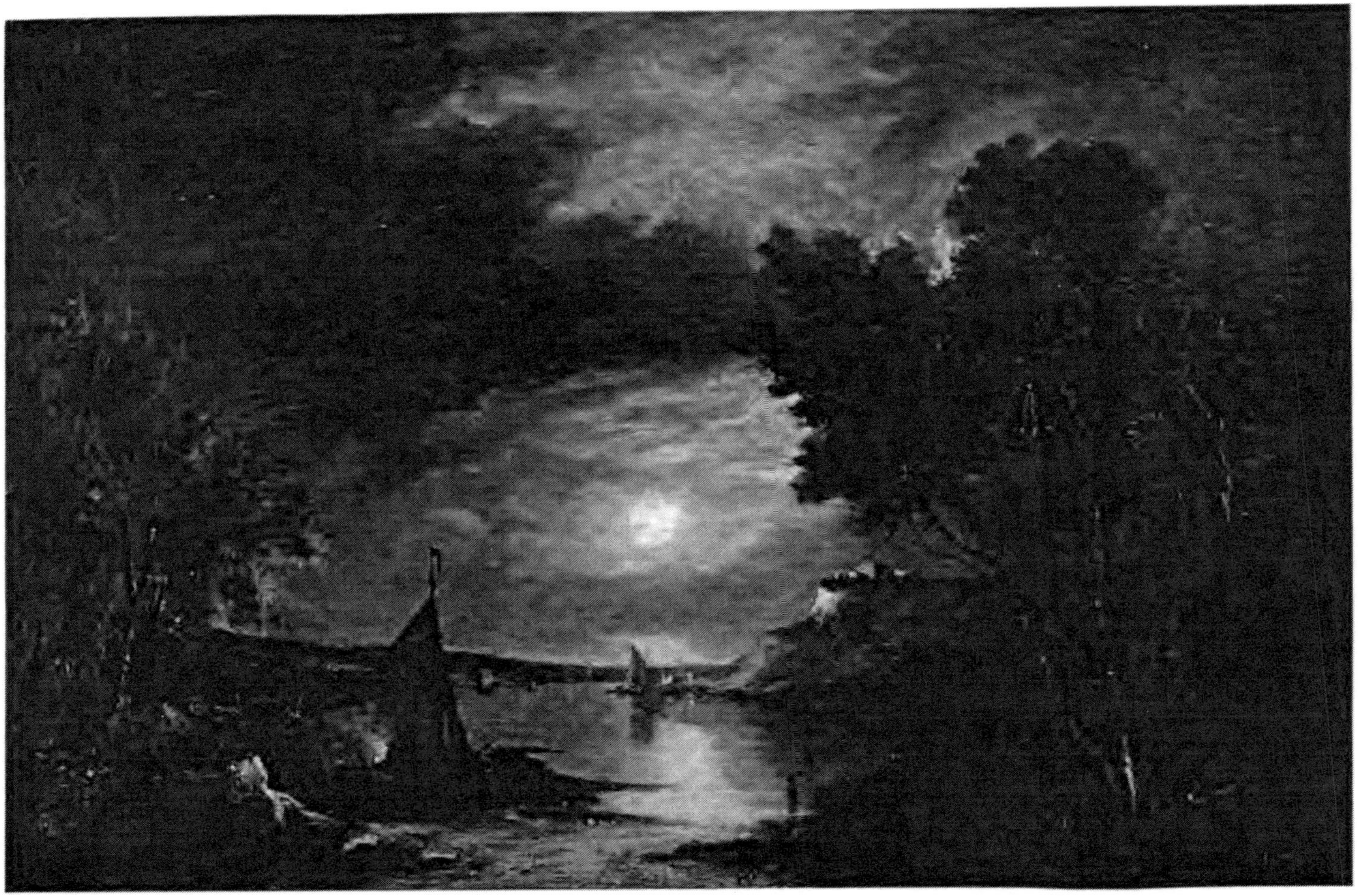

(In the possession of Russell J. Colman, Esq.)

"RIVER SCENE BY MOONLIGHT." OIL PAINTING BY JOHN BERNEY CROME (17 × 11½ INCHES)

PLATE LXIV

LANDSCAPE OIL PAINTING BY JOHN BERNEY LADBROOKE (36 × 24 INCHES)

(In the Castle Museum, Norwich)

PLATE LXV

"THE SLUICE GATE." OIL PAINTING BY JOHN BERNEY LADBROOKE (29⅛ × 19¾ INCHES)

(In the possession of Russell J. Colman, Esq)

PLATE LXVI

"OLD FISH MARKET, NORWICH." OIL PAINTING BY DAVID HODGSON (34½ × 28½ INCHES)

(In the possession of Russell J. Colman, Esq.)

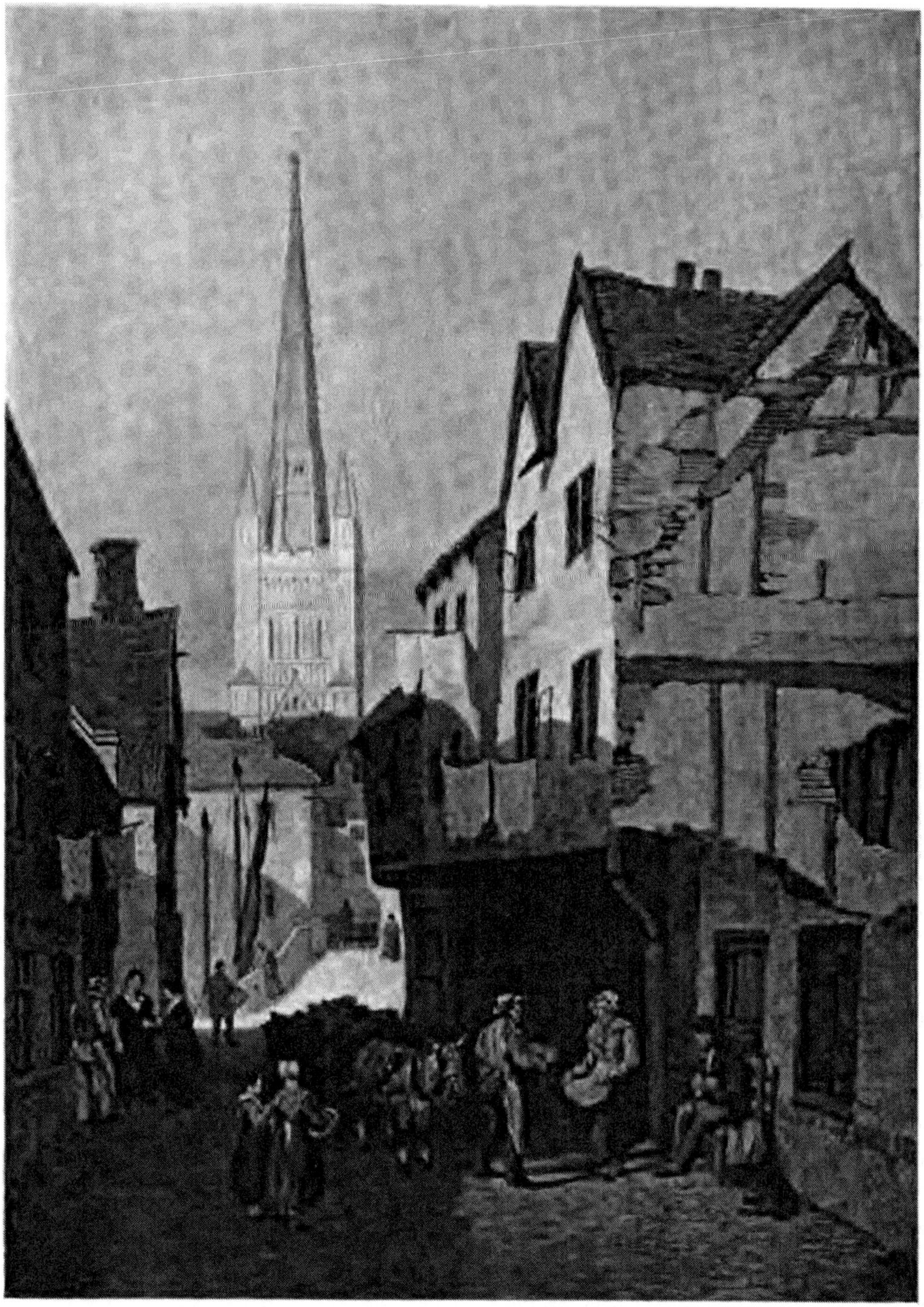

(In the possession of Russell J. Colman, Esq.)

"FISHGATE STREET, NORWICH." OIL PAINTING BY HENRY NINHAM (10¼ × 13¼ INCHES)

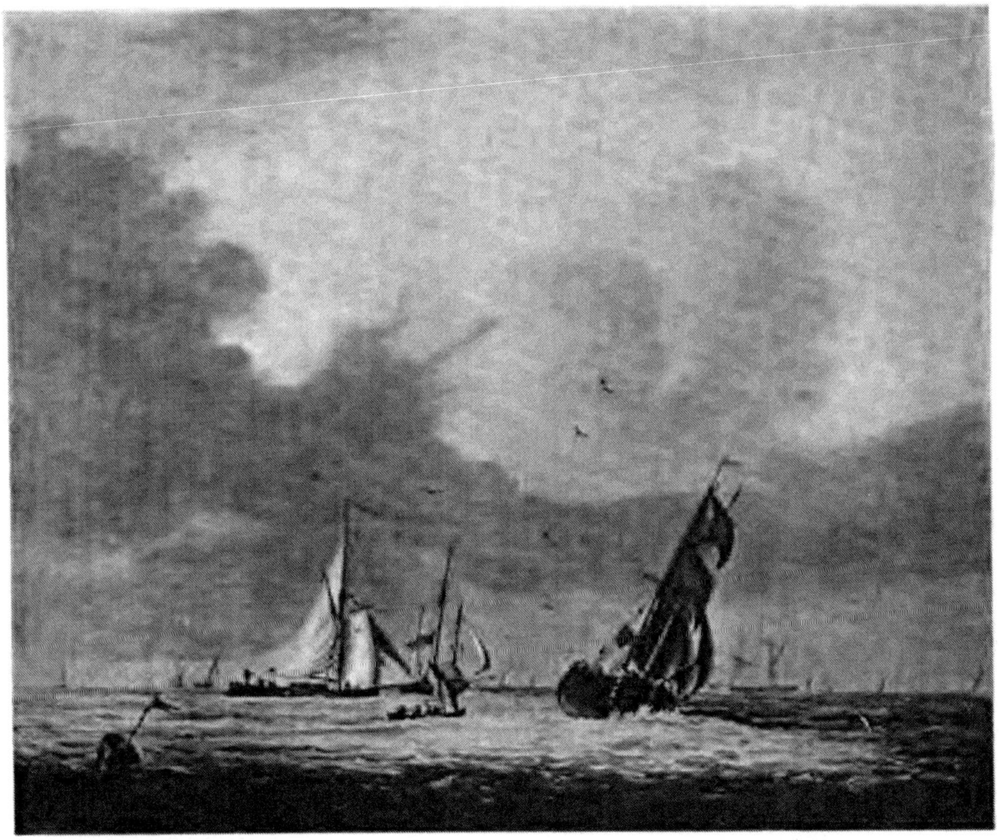

(In the possession of Arthur Michael Samuel, Esq., M.P.)

"FISHING BOATS." OIL PAINTING BY JOSEPH STANNARD (18½ × 15 INCHES)

PLATE XV

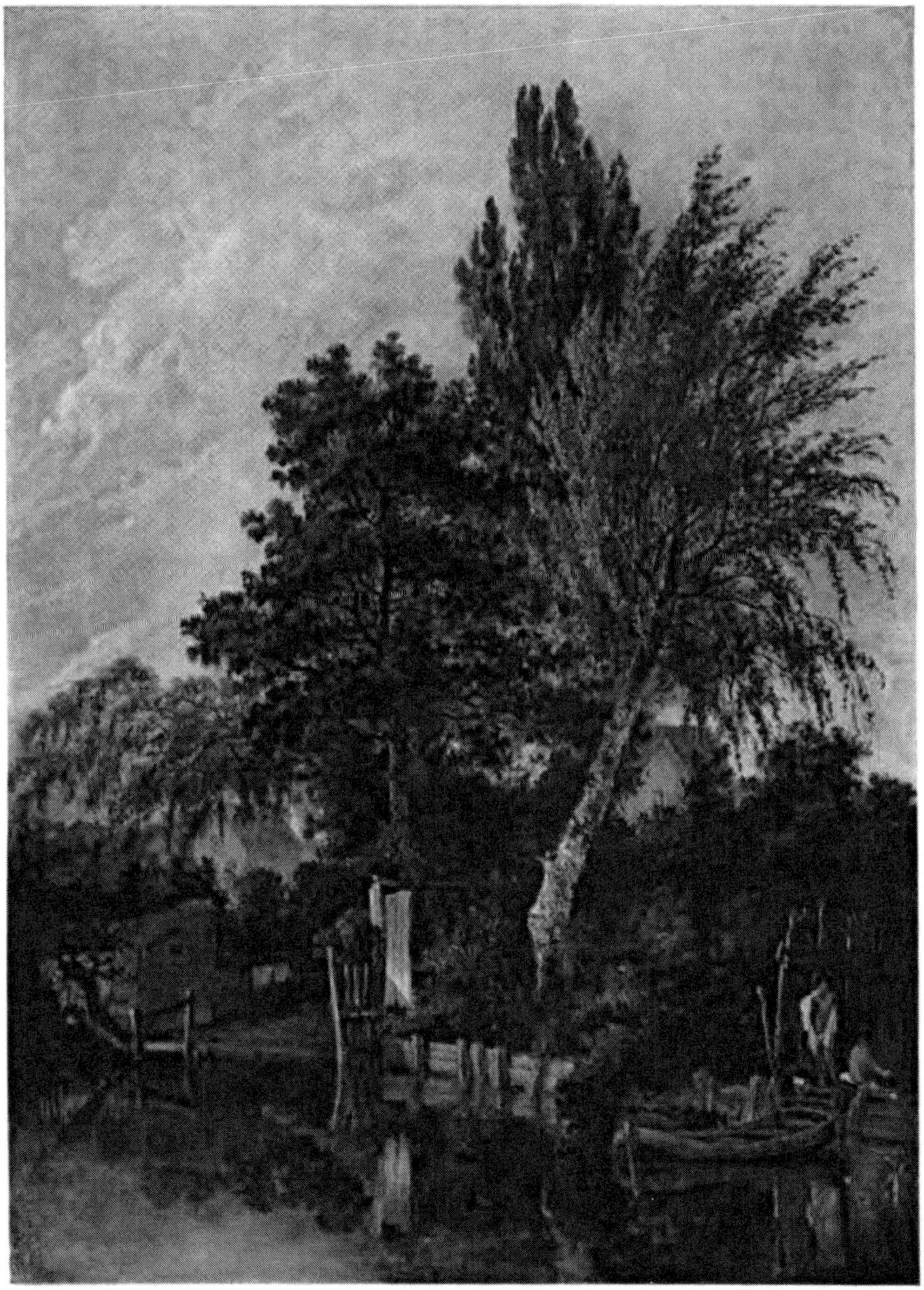

(In the possession of H. Darell-Brown, Esq.)

"A BATHING SCENE—VIEW ON THE WENSUM AT THORPE, NORWICH." OIL PAINTING BY JOHN CROME (13¾ × 18½ INCHES)

PLATE LXIX

(*In the possession of*
Russell J. Colman, Esq.)

"YARMOUTH JETTY." OIL PAINTING BY
ALFRED STANNARD (16 × 12½ INCHES)

PLATE LXX

"WHITLINGHAM REACH." WATER-COLOUR BY JOHN THIRTLE (30½ × 18¾ INCHES)

(In the possession of Russell J. Colman, Esq.)

PLATE LXXI

(*In the British Museum, London*)

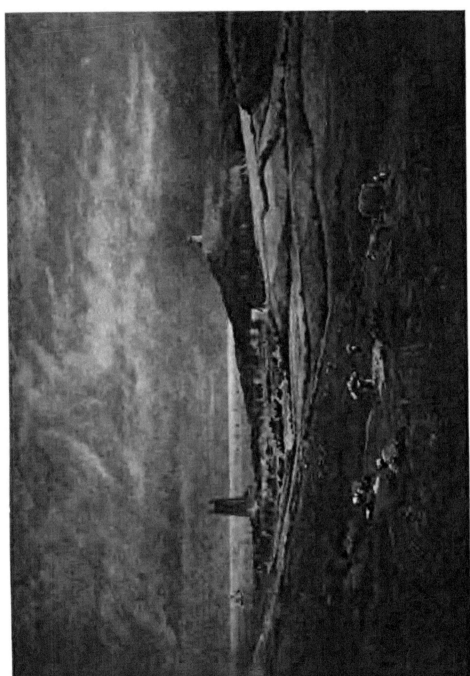

"CROMER, LOOKING EAST." WATER-COLOUR BY JOHN THIRTLE (13¾ × 10 INCHES)

PLATE LXXII

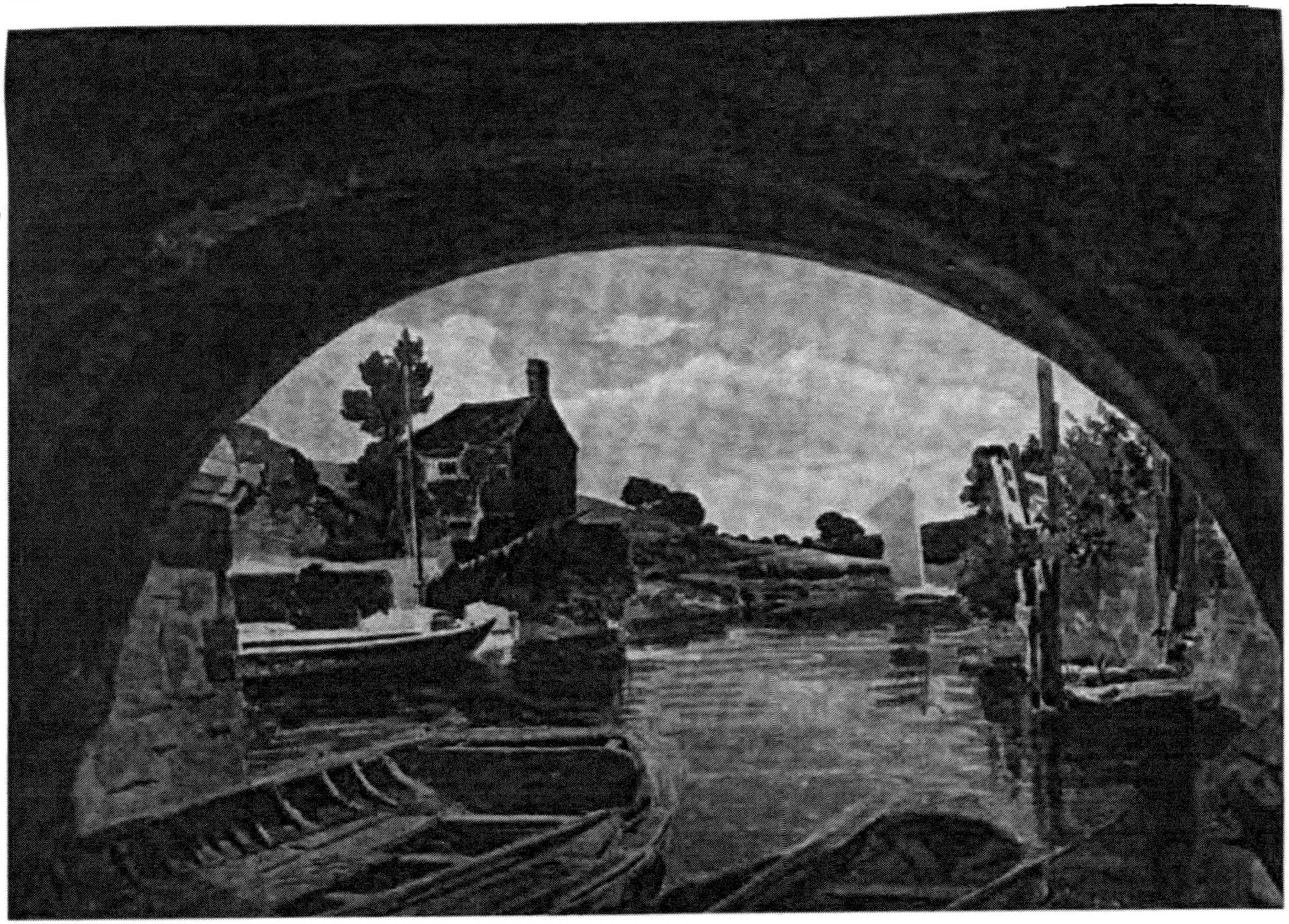

(*In the British Museum, London*)

"VIEW UNDER BISHOP'S BRIDGE, NORWICH." WATER-COLOUR BY JOHN THIRTLE (15⅞ × 11¼ INCHES)

PLATE LXXIII

"ST MAGNUS'S CHURCH, LONDON BRIDGE, AND NEIGHBOURING BUILDINGS." WATER-COLOUR BY JOHN THIRTLE (19¼ × 13¼ INCHES)

(*In the Victoria and Albert Museum, London*)

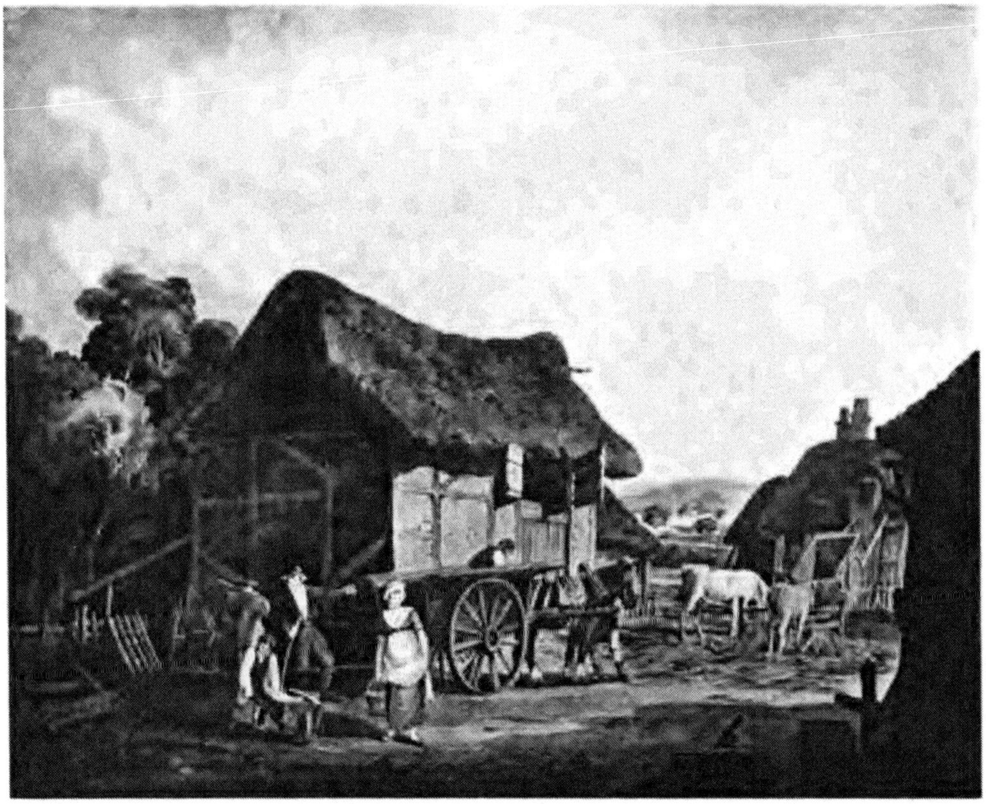

(In the Victoria and Albert Museum, London)

"THE FARMYARD." WATER-COLOUR BY ROBERT DIXON (28 × 22½ INCHES)

PLATE LXXV

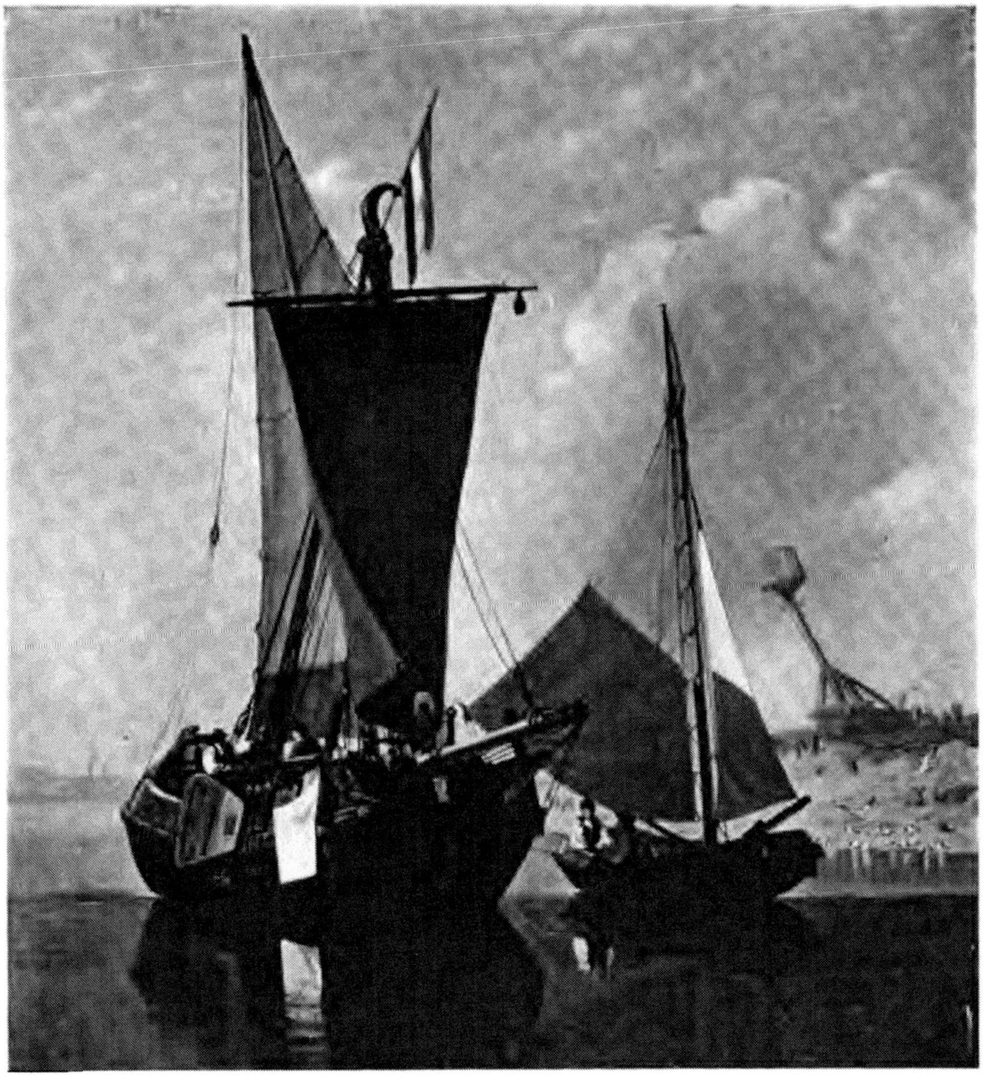

*(In the Castle Museum, Norwich
Colman Bequest)*

"BOATS ON THE MEDWAY." OIL
PAINTING BY MILES EDMUND
COTMAN ($19\frac{1}{2} \times 21\frac{1}{2}$ INCHES)

PLATE LXXVI

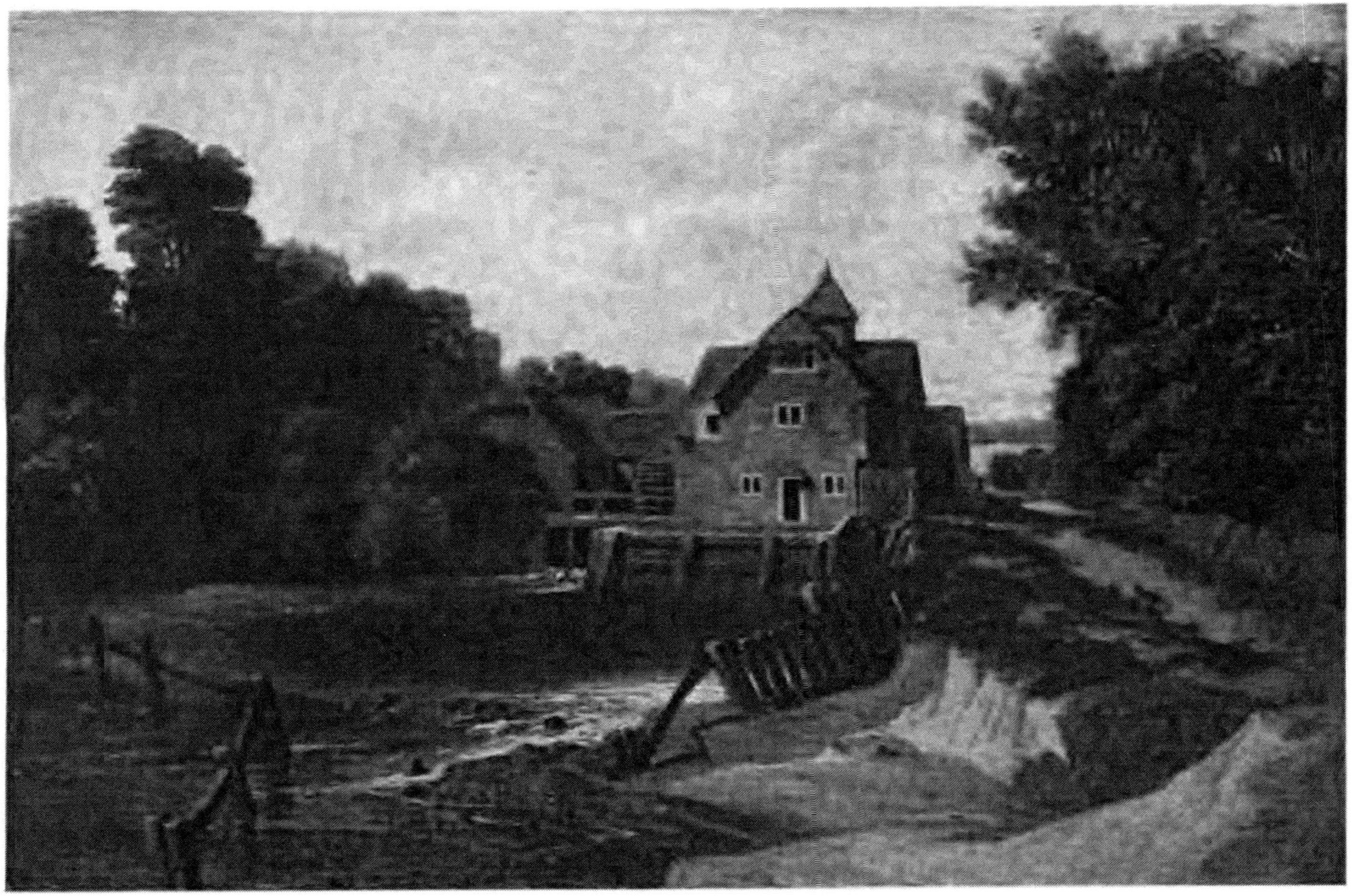

(In the possession of Russell J. Colman, Esq.)

"TROWSE MILLS." OIL PAINTING BY MILES EDMUND COTMAN (19 × 13 INCHES)

PLATE LXXVII

(*In the Castle Museum, Norwich*)

"WHITLINGHAM, LOOKING TOWARDS NORWICH." WATER-COLOUR BY JOHN JOSEPH COTMAN (26¾ × 14¼ INCHES)

PLATE LXXVIII

"ELY CATHEDRAL." WATER-COLOUR BY THOMAS LOUND (24½ × 12½ INCHES)

(In the Castle Museum, Norwich)

PLATE LXXIX

"ST. BENET'S ABBEY." OIL PAINTING BY THOMAS LOUND (29¼ × 17¼ INCHES)

(In the possession of Russell J. Colman, Esq.)

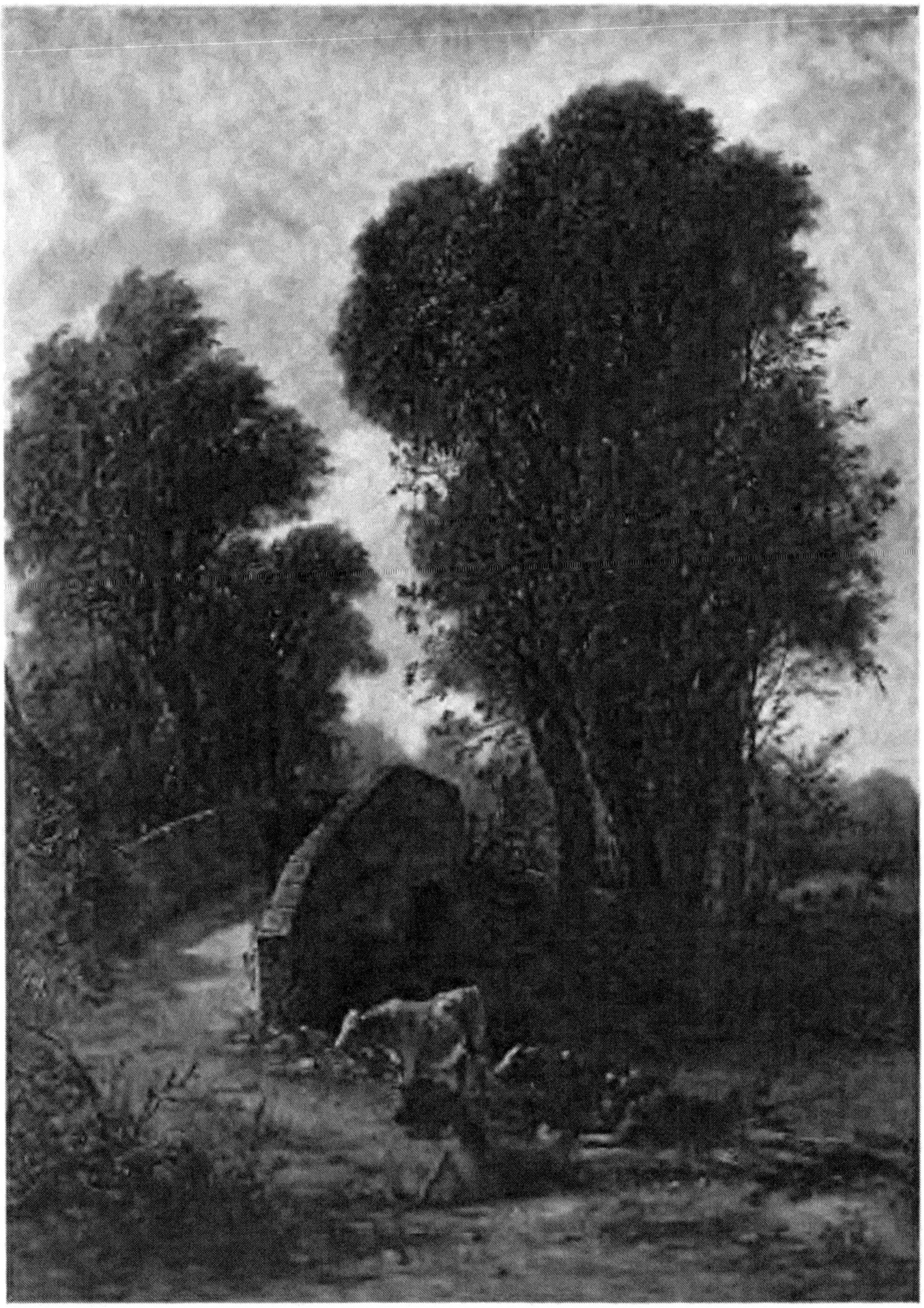

(*In the possession of Russell J. Colman, Esq.*)

"GODSTOW BRIDGE, OXFORD." OIL PAINTING BY ALFRED PRIEST (21¼ × 29¼ INCHES)

CPSIA information can be obtained at www.ICGtesting.com
Printed in the USA
BVOW051206200612

293224BV00003B/12/P